Ruff Love

Susan Garrett

A Relationship-Building Program for You and Your Dog

Clean Run

South Hadley, Massachusetts, U.S.A.

Ruff Love: A Relationship Building Program for You and Your Dog

Copyright © 2002, 2009 by Susan Garrett

All rights reserved. No part of this book may be used or reproduced in any form or by any means electronic or mechanical including photocopying, recording, or by any information storage or retrieval system, without the prior written permission of the publisher.

For information contact:
Clean Run Productions, LLC
17 Industrial Dr.
South Hadley, MA 01075
Phone: 413-532-1389 or 800-311-6503
Email: info@cleanrun.com
Website: www.cleanrun.com

Book design and typesetting by Monica Percival

Cover design by Anne Cusolito

Cover Photo by Digital Vision® Ltd.

Illustrations by Tweenergraphics

Trademarks: All service marks, trademarks, and product names used in this publication belong to their respective holders.

First printing 2002

ISBN 978-1-892694-06-5

Printed in the U.S.A.

Dedication

For Shelby, Speki, Stoni, Twister, Buzz, and DeCaff

*The greatest teachers any dog trainer
could ever hope to have.*

About Susan Garrett

Susan Garrett's interest in animal behavior started at the University of Guelph where she earned a BSc in Animal Science. Since then she has developed into a pre-eminent canine sports instructor and competitor. Each dog Susan has competed with in agility has made at least one appearance in the finals of a national event, and her dogs have won 11 different National Agility Championships since 1996. Susan has been a member of a world record-holding flyball team for eight consecutive years. In addition, she is one of Canada's top obedience competitors; each of the four dogs she has trialed has earned at least one High In Trial award. Susan's understanding of the use of operant conditioning to train dogs and teach people has earned her worldwide recognition. She has shown people how to apply clicker training in canine competition throughout North America and as far away as Japan. Her dogs perform with a happy attitude and great precision, enjoying their work as much as Susan enjoys working with them. A natural teacher and an entertaining speaker, Susan loves dogs and loves helping others achieve a special relationship with their dogs. Susan shares her life with John Blenkey in Alberton, Ontario, Canada and their six dogs—Border Collies: Stoni, Buzz, and Quid; and Jack Russell Terriers: Shelby, Twister, and DeCaff.

Table of Contents

Acknowledgements

Ruff Love represents the experience I have gained by living with, working with, being frustrated by, and loving dogs that each have had their own unique set of challenges. I am eternally grateful for having been given the chance to own six "once in a lifetime" dogs.

A book such as this never comes from the talents of one person. I would like to thank the people who have contributed in one way or another to its development.

I am grateful for the knowledge I have gleaned from many gifted trainers. They have all helped to mold my perception as a dog trainer. I feel honored to have had the opportunity to learn from Terri Arnold, Bob Bailey, the late Marion Breland Bailey, Karen Pryor, and Gary Wilkes. Since we all learn from everyone we meet, I am sure there are people who have influenced my dog training whom I have unfortunately overlooked. If this includes you, please know that I appreciate all the insight that you have shared with me and I thank you.

I am truly blessed to have what I humbly consider to be the greatest staff of dog trainers in the world. By working together we learn from each other. Many thanks to Mary Ellen Barry, Barb DeMascio,

Val Dillon, Ruth Hunt, Kathy Keats, Mary Ann Kras, Nancy Ouellette, Jen Pinder, and Theresa Rector. This group of amazingly talented instructors blends together dog-training ability, athleticism, people skills, and teaching insight. Clearly, they are the reason *Say Yes Dog Training* is as successful as it is today. I am not only proud to call them friends, but also grateful to them for all their many talents. Their input into our program has added immeasurably to the content of this book.

A special thank you to those who have done the painstaking job of editing this book (over and over again). I am putting their names in print, so let's hope they didn't mess up in any big way. Thank you to Bill and Susan Brereton, Kathy Keats, Mary Ann Kras, Nancy Ouellette, Anne Stocum, Ruth Hunt, and Michele Stone.

A heartfelt thanks also goes out to Monica Percival and the Clean Run staff for all of the hours put in to get this book into print.

I would be remiss if I didn't take the chance to acknowledge all of the students who have trained with us over the years. They and their dogs have presented challenges that inspired us to look for new alternatives in the field of training dogs and teaching people. We are not successful unless they are successful. Each pupil helps us to build a better program for tomorrow's students. Thank you one and all.

Clearly, the one person that I have grown to rely on the most is my spouse and the co-owner of *Say Yes Dog Training*, John Blenkey. John's exemplary work ethic is nothing short of inspiring. His unconditional support of all that I do is more than any one person really deserves.

Chapter One
Does My Dog Need "Ruff Love?"

Dogs do what is reinforcing. If a dog is allowed the freedom to choose what is most rewarding to him, he always will. People may call this dog "independent"; we can call this dog "a dog." The truth is, many of the dogs that need the Ruff Love program are as "normal" as the next dog. They have simply learned how to get what they want from their owners. Rather than the owner training the dog, the dog has successfully trained the owner! Candidates for the Ruff Love program include:

- Dogs currently labeled "stupid," "spiteful," "bad," "stubborn," "spirited," "independent," "untrainable," "unmotivated," or just "unresponsive."

- Aggressive dogs or dogs who need behavior modification.

- Performance dogs with whom the handler wants to share a better "working" relationship.

- Rescue dogs or puppies going into their new homes.

Anyone who feels that his or her relationship with a dog is not quite as good as it could be, will reap benefits from the Ruff Love program.

Aggressive Dogs and Ruff Love

If you have an aggressive dog, the Ruff Love program will help your dog develop the confidence he needs to overcome his fears and it will give you an understanding of how to defuse potentially disruptive situations.

Performance-Sports Dogs and Ruff Love

If you compete in canine sports (such as agility, obedience, flyball, freestyle, tracking, etc.), your performance will benefit from a strong working relationship with your dog. Perhaps you find it difficult to motivate your dog to do what you would like him to do, when you would like him to do it. Perhaps your competition dog is "too energetic" or "too distracted" to give you his best work. Your competition dog may not be the kind of partner you had hoped for, but that can be changed. The Ruff Love program is designed to alter your dog's environment so that you control all of the reinforcement he receives. The program will show you where you may be catering to your dog's demands and inadvertently reinforcing the very behaviors you want to eliminate!

Puppies and Ruff Love

Your new puppy came home and it was love at first sight for both of you. Unfortunately, of late, the adoration and respect does not always appear to be mutual. You have given your puppy everything he could ever want, but it seems that he does not look to you as the main source of fun in his life. Although, your puppy hangs around with you when there is nothing better around to stimulate him, the moment another dog appears or squirrels are nearby to chase, you are no longer quite as important to him. The modified Ruff Love for Puppies program described in Chapter Six will assist you in developing a great bond with your puppy and raising a dog that looks to you as his number one source of all good things.

Recall Problems and Ruff Love

How does your dog respond when you call him? Does he come to you only because he is intimidated by what you might "do" to him? Does he choose not to come if he is playing far away from you? When you call him, is his response slow and labored? Does he come only after he has checked out all nearby

distractions? Do you often need to call him more than once before he responds? Do you have to scream and shout before he notices you? Do you occasionally have to shake the cookie can, or pretend you have a treat, to get him to come? Are there times when your dog acts as if he can't hear you? Does he choose not to come when other dogs are running and playing nearby? The reliability of your recall is a good way to measure the relationship between you and your dog. If you answered "yes" to any of the questions above, your relationship needs strengthening. The Ruff Love program will help you to achieve just that.

The Program Motto

"Positive is not permissive" will become a mantra to you. Many people try to train "positively," but often, the dog trained using positive methods ends up a spoiled, self-rewarding nuisance. Training in a positive way is effective if you are successful in limiting the rewards your dog receives from his environment. To effect a change in his behavior and in your relationship, you need to stop being a pushover to your dog's demands and start applying the laws of how dogs learn. By reinforcing desired behaviors and eliminating the opportunity for inappropriate behaviors, you will shape your dog into a well-rounded companion or competition partner.

Chapter Two
How Long Does the Program Last?

Your dog's progress determines the length of the Ruff Love program.
The curriculum is divided into four progressive stages which are described in Chapters Seven through Ten. The length of each stage depends upon the effort of the trainer and the responses of the dog. Most mature dogs need a minimum of 10 weeks to work through Stages One and Two; expect to add some privileges back to your dog's life after five to six weeks. If you are starting with a puppy, you will not apply Stage Two until the puppy is approximately seven months old; you will continue the program until your puppy reaches one year of age.

Be aware that there are some essential elements of the program that must be maintained for the lifetime of your dog. These are discussed in Chapter Four.

During the Ruff Love program you can still enjoy many of the same activities you previously did with your dog. However, he will learn that all of the things *he* expected, whenever *he* decided to have them, will no longer be available to him on his terms. As you start the Ruff Love program, you will radically change your dog's environment by making sure that he:

- is crated when not interacting with you.
- experiences all free time and exercise on a leash or long line.
- is not allowed on any furniture.
- is hand fed his meals by you.
- does not have toys left out in his environment, only chew bones.
- plays with toys only when interacting with you.
- only plays with other dogs when you are frequently calling him back to you. If your recall is not yet good enough for this, the dog should not be allowed off-leash access to other dogs.
- has no free time in the back yard to romp and do as he pleases. This means boarding up your dog door if you own one.
- continuously wears a head halter when out of his crate.
- receives nothing for "free." All rewards—attention, toys, treats, etc.—are earned.

It is likely that you will see an increase in your dog's focus for his work and for you within a few weeks of starting the program. But do *not* be tempted to stop there. With most dogs, for a permanent change to occur, you need to be committed to the Ruff Love program for at least 12-16 weeks and get through to Stage Four. For best results, you need to apply *all* the elements of the program, not just the ones that are convenient for you.

Be wary of adding back privileges too soon as this is detrimental to the possibility of permanent change. Your dog may not have been reinforced sufficiently for the newer, more appropriate responses to become *habit*. As a result, your dog will slide back to his previously reinforcing, undesired behavior. You will then need to revisit Stage One of the program and you will find that the second time around you need to keep your dog on the program much longer.

It is always best to be cautious in rating your progress and to stick to the suggested length for each stage right from the start.

Chapter Three
The Role of the Ruff Love Trainer

The trainer's commitment determines the level of success the dog achieves with Ruff Love. You need to take responsibility for the relationship that you have with your dog. You need to accept the fact that your dog is a reflection of your abilities as a trainer. Any skill your dog performs well shows an area of training where you have been a good trainer. Conversely, poorly developed skills in your dog reveal areas in your training where you lack understanding. Be committed to seek out the knowledge you require to develop the skills you need to educate your dog.

While working through the Ruff Love program, it is crucial that you be:

- consistent with your implementation of each stage.

- fair to your dog.

- conscious of maintaining a high rate of reinforcement when training new skills.

Life as your dog currently knows it needs to end today; tomorrow, life will consist of a very different picture. In your dog's "new world," you will reinforce him for appropriate behaviors and you won't give him the opportunity to choose other, socially unacceptable behaviors. For puppies and rescue dogs coming into a new home, the implementation of this program is much easier, as there is no history to work against.

If you are determined to develop a strong relationship with your dog, you need to follow the Ruff Love curriculum with exactness. All of your dog's privileges will be stripped away and then added back, one by one, as he *earns* them. The following suggestions may seem overwhelming, and nearly impossible to apply, but they are nonetheless *all* necessary for your relationship rebuilding program to succeed. These suggestions may seem severe because you love your dog and want him to be happy, but consider this: You would not give your teenager, who just learned to drive, the keys to a new Porsche. Responsibility like that needs to be earned as the adolescent matures and proves he is trustworthy. Likewise, you need to curtail the freedom you offer your dog until he has been reinforced enough to make the decisions you want to see him make.

Try to imagine your lifestyle if your dog had suffered an injury. Prolonged crate rest and leash walking would be necessary for healing. You would never think of that kind of restriction as "severe," but rather "necessary." You need to accept the fact that your dog *has* suffered an injury: in this case, an emotional injury rather than a physical one. You need to limit the privileges your dog currently enjoys in order to allow the healing to begin.

Puppies in the Ruff Love for Puppies program also need to have their freedom restricted. This allows your puppy to grow up in an environment where he is seldom wrong, since he is rarely given the opportunity to choose an inappropriate response.

The restrictions your dog is about to experience will allow you to control everything that he finds rewarding. Up until now, you may not have realized how many rewards your dog has been "stealing" without your knowledge: chasing squirrels, cats, or shadows in the yard; jumping on guests; raiding the trash; digging in the garden; demanding affection from you; wrestling with your other dogs or kids; enjoying the plethora of toys you have given him; sleeping on the furniture; tugging on his leash; playing with water from the hose; or barking at people on the street (the list is endless). These are all examples of reinforcement your dog may be taking whenever he chooses. You may eventually choose to continue to reinforce any of these behaviors, but the Ruff Love program will enable you to do so on your terms, when you determine it is appropriate.

Follow the Ruff Love program without lapses or exceptions and you will be rewarded with a dog that has a solid understanding of how he can *earn* reinforcement from *you!*

Build Up Conditioned Reinforcers

A **conditioned reinforcer** is a **stimulus** (anything currently in your dog's environment) that initially has no particular meaning to your dog. By pairing a stimulus, such as a noise or a signal, with something your dog really loves, he learns that the noise or signal means a reward is coming. Your first assigned task is to train your dog to respond to three conditioned reinforcers:

- A **clicker**—A training device that consists of a small, plastic box with a metal strip that makes a sharp, clicking sound when pushed and released.

- A word

- A finger point

Throughout your training, you will need a conditioned reinforcer to "mark" appropriate behavior in your dog. A clicker is the best one to start with, since most dogs quickly make the association between the click and the reward. Here are a few fundamentals:

- Click your clicker and give your dog a highly-valued treat like steak or cheese or a game of tug (if that is what he really enjoys). Do this until your dog reacts in a joyful, expectant manner each time you click.

- Now build up the reward value of a word like "yes" in the same way. Say "yes" and then reward your dog with a treat or toy.

- The last conditioned reinforcer to build up is a finger point. There may be times when you want to quietly reward your dog for good behavior; for example, perhaps there is another dog nearby who knows what a click or the word "yes" means and you want to single out good behavior in your dog without disrupting the other dogs. The finger point is also a good choice if you have your dog with you in a room full of other people or if he is on the other side of the room. Condition the finger point just as you did the clicker and the word "yes," by pointing your finger at your dog and then rewarding him with a highly-valued treat or toy.

Stand Your Ground

No exceptions can be made to the program if you sincerely hope to turn things around. Your dog needs to live a far more structured existence; one where you control all of his choices.

Be Confident, Decisive, and Fair

You must be a confident decision-maker for your dog or puppy so that he is less likely to think that he needs to control his environment—this is particularly true for aggressive dogs.

Control Reinforcements

You must control anything that is stimulating to your dog in his environment. Pay attention to the less obvious reinforcements the dog is obtaining when he displays socially unacceptable behavior. Opportunities for him to find reinforcements without your controlling them need to be eliminated. Your dog may be obsessively staring at objects in motion, such as other dogs, cars, or children. He may be staring, lip curling, lunging, or snapping at a "target." If your dog is off leash, you cannot control the reinforcement your dog receives by engaging in these undesirable behaviors. To punish afterward does not alter the reward value already received by your dog. You need to employ good behavioral management until you can effect a change in what is causing these responses.

While your dog is with you, he will always be on a head halter and a leash. You must watch his eyes and read his body language so that you can redirect his attention before he becomes fixated on a target. You must apply a schedule of rapid reinforcement in order to keep your dog's attention on you until you can get him away from the target of his inappropriate attention.

Reinforcing Correct Responses

Rate of reinforcement (RR) is the number of correct responses that you reward during a minute of training with your dog. To document your rate of reinforcement, you need to keep track of the *number of rewards* your dog gets during each training session as well as the *length of each session*. For example, if you trained your dog for 5 minutes and you gave him 5 tug sessions and 25 treats during the session, your rate of reinforcement is 6 rewards per minute—30 (rewards) divided by 5 (minutes of training). From this, you could then deduce that your dog had to wait an average 10 seconds (60 seconds divided by 6 rewards) between each reward you gave him.

Your dog's rate of reinforcement is dependent upon many factors, such as:

- How adept you are at delivering the reward immediately after the click—if it consistently takes you time to deliver the reward, the dog's rate of reinforcement will be lower.

- How much time it takes the dog to eat the type of treat you gave him—if it takes the dog time to "crunch up" the treats to eat them, his rate of reinforcement will be lower.

- Where you are standing in relation to where your dog is working—if the dog needs to travel a long way to receive his reward, his rate of reinforcement will be lower.

- If you use toys as a reward during your training session—although a tug session may last for 30 or more seconds, it still counts as only one reward received by the dog, therefore his rate of reinforcement will be lower.

- How long it takes the dog to perform the skill you are hoping to see—if the skill itself takes 30 seconds to accomplish, it will reduce the number of rewards your dog receives during a five-minute training session.

When you are initially teaching a new skill to your dog, you should aim for a reinforcement rate of *at least* 20-30 clicks and rewards per minute. To accomplish this, you need to use food more often than toys as rewards in your training sessions. As your dog gets more proficient at the skill you are teaching, your rate of reinforcement can be lower and you can use more toys and tug sessions to reinforce correct responses.

Maintain a High Success Rate

Be certain to maintain a high success rate during training sessions with your Ruff Love dog. Identify your dog's **success rate** by keeping track of the total number of responses (both the ones you reward and the ones you do *not* reward) during each training session. Divide the *number of responses you reward* by your *dog's total number of responses* to get your success rate for that training session. For example, if your dog offered you 25 responses during your training session and you rewarded 10 of the responses, your success rate would be .4 or 40%—10 (responses you rewarded) divided by 25 (total responses).

During any training session, try to have your dog be successful at least 70-80% of the time. This means that you are only allowing your dog to fail 20-30% of the time while working with you. Your success rate can drop to 30-40% during any one training session, as long as you are conscientious in your other training sessions to allow your dog to be more successful. Over the course of the week, your success rate should average around 80%.

After each training session, make an effort to document your dog's rate of reinforcement and success rate. If your rate of reinforcement is high enough, you will see a corresponding high success rate. If your rate of reinforcement is low, your dog's success rate for that training session will also be low.

- If you have a low success rate for several consecutive training sessions, your dog will not be as enthusiastic about his work. If your dog is not excited about his work, he is not likely to offer you as many responses the next time you train.

If your dog offers fewer responses, there is less chance for you to reinforce him; therefore, your rate of reinforcement will fall further.

- If your dog must wait too long between rewards, he may start to show **anxiety behaviors** such as barking, spinning, yawning, or whining among others. Soon your dog may even "shut down" or stop working. Because the dog has seen little opportunity to earn reinforcement, he will stop offering you responses.

To avoid either of these situations, be conscientious of maintaining a high rate of reinforcement and a high success rate in your training. This means you must be sure the criteria you have selected for your dog are realistic and achievable for his level of training. Ensure a higher success rate by asking for easier behaviors or moving your dog further away from distractions when working.

By monitoring your rate of reinforcement and your success rate, you can observe the impact they have on your dog's performance and his attitude toward working with you.

Give Time-Outs for Inappropriate Behaviors

You will give your dog **time-outs** when he displays inappropriate behaviors. These time-outs can be as minimal as turning your back on your dog (providing the behavior he is offering is not self-rewarding), gently turning his head away from a distraction while he is on a leash and head halter, or picking up the food or toy you are training with and putting it away. Alternatively, you may ask your dog to sit or down for his time-out or put him in his crate.

It is best to mix up the form the time-out takes so that a location or body position doesn't become associated with the time-out.

Time-outs are **negative punishment**; you are taking the dog away from something he finds rewarding or taking away the opportunity for reinforcement. Even though they are a form of punishment, time-outs should be delivered in a *neutral* manner. You must be unemotional when you give a time-out. Your voice should be pleasant and calm, if you are talking at all.

Do not overuse time-outs, since they can become very frustrating for your dog. Never give a dog a time-out if you have not first given ample reinforcement for the alternate behavior you want from your dog. If a dog receives a time-out without knowing how to act appropriately, you cannot expect his behavior to change.

You must evaluate the effectiveness of time-outs on an ongoing basis. If your dog continues to display an inappropriate response, review your reinforcement history. You need to balance all time-outs with lots of opportunity for reinforcement the next time you give the dog your attention. If you are giving many time-outs for the same behavior (more than 25%), it should be a "red flag" that your dog does not understand how to be correct. Make it easier by altering your criteria or moving to a less-distracting environment, so your dog can achieve a higher success rate. You might also try rapid firing rewards to your dog before he has a chance to be wrong. **Rapid firing** means that you continuously give your dog treats, as fast as you can, so that he does not notice a distraction nearby.

Time-Out Reminders

- Time-outs should be used only in an environment rich with positive reinforcement: do not repeatedly give a dog a time-out for the same inappropriate behavior, as this can be frustrating for both you and your dog.

- Apply time-outs using different body positions or locations. Do not fall into the habit of using only one location for your time-outs (such as a crate), since this can become a location your dog will want to avoid (all dogs should feel safe and secure in their crates).

- Execute the time-outs without emotion. Do not be upset or even think unhappy thoughts. Use a neutral voice as you give a time-out.

- Do not overuse time-outs. If the dog continues to make the same mistake, go back and train; it is likely your dog does not completely understand what you are asking him to do.

Positive Is Not Permissive

It is critical that you understand the difference between a trainer whose foundation of training is "positive reinforcement" and a trainer who is permissive with his or her dog. The permissive dog owner often has a spoiled dog that does what he wants when he wants. This is not the case with a good trainer who chooses to train in a positive way. If you cue the dog for a behavior, you must follow up on your request each and every time. Dogs will always do what is reinforcing to them. If you heavily reinforce your dog when he behaves as he should, his good behavior is likely to be repeated. There must never be any uncertainty in your mind about how you would like your dog to behave at any given moment. Be clear and consistent with your expectations. Any ambiguity on your part will result in an incomplete understanding on the part of the dog.

Always keep in mind that the rewards your dog receives from his environment can be more reinforcing than those you are delivering. It is up to you to be in control of *everything* that reinforces your dog.

Chapter Four
Essential Elements for All Stages of Ruff Love

The following "essential elements" are the program criteria that you will put into practice today and that you will maintain throughout, and beyond, the Ruff Love program. Being consistent with your implementation of these guidelines allows good habits to become a lifetime routine for both you and your dog.

All Behaviors Have a Consequence

The dog that has been allowed to grab a toy from you whenever he wanted has been reinforcing himself with this inappropriate behavior. Knowing that all behaviors have a consequence, you can see why your dog has continued with this and other annoying behaviors. When the outcome is a good one, any behavior may be repeated. You are now going to turn this around and show your dog a different consequence to his behaviors.

Be prepared ahead of time to reward the behaviors you would like to see repeated and to give a time-out for those antics you deem undesirable.

For example, suppose that when you arrive home from work, your overexuberant dog wants to jump up on you. You can choose to apply one of two consequences:

- You can scold the dog or knee him in the chest as many dog trainers advocate. However, this is very likely rewarding the behavior that you are trying to eliminate because the dog who jumps on people is only trying to seek out personal attention. Your scolding this dog is giving him the attention he desires.

- Alternatively, you can give him a subtle time-out by saying nothing to this happy dog and turning away from the dog toward the wall. The dog may try to jump on your back, but if you continue to ignore his inappropriate behavior, he is likely to try something new (such as a sit or down) to get your attention. At the moment he sits, you can turn around and say "hello" to him. If he attempts to jump on you again, once again turn and face the wall, giving the dog exactly the opposite of what he wants.

It may require creative thinking on your part to design an appropriate response such as this to all of the behaviors your dog is currently exhibiting.

As with training any response in your dog (or kids!), consistency is the key to success. If you maintain consistent boundaries for your dog's appropriate behavior, he will start to respect the boundaries you have set up for him.

Dogs Are Not Allowed on the Furniture

Your dog should no longer be given the opportunity to get up on furniture. The dog that jumps on and off the sofa or your bed is taking a huge environmental reinforcement whenever he wants. You must eliminate this reward. Extensive reinforcements for lying in dog beds will help, but keeping your dog on leash around the house may be necessary to avoid scolding him for getting up on the furniture. Through reinforcement, he will gain an understanding of how his household rules have changed.

This rule need not be a lifetime commitment, but rather one that you may want to apply for the next year or so of his life. Because this rule is difficult to enforce at night, you must have your dog sleep in his crate. You may choose to have the crate beside your bed so he can be near you, helping to develop your relationship further while you sleep!

You Must Control Environmental Reinforcements

Once a behavior has been reinforced, the probability of it being repeated increases. This is the reason many dogs learn to steal food from the garbage: it is reinforcing for them to do so. But food is not the only reward that a dog can earn. Shredding a toy, chasing another animal, or digging a hole are examples of environmental rewards that may be as reinforcing to some dogs as a big chunk of meat. By becoming aware of all the activities that your dog finds rewarding, you can either eliminate them (like chasing cars) or use them as rewards while training (like getting to play with the water hose).

You Must Identify Action-Prompting Behaviors

Action-prompting behaviors are responses your dog has learned will earn him reinforcement from the subject he is soliciting. A dog that play-bows in front of another dog is often rewarded by that dog running and playing with him. A dog that jumps on a house guest is rewarded with the attention of the guest (even if it is a scolding, it is attention). Try to imagine that your dog has a language all his own. When jumping on your guest, it's as if he is saying, *"Yo, dude. Here I am. Pat me!"* A more appropriate response from your dog would be for him to sit in front of your guest as if to say, *"Look at me being a good boy. Mother-may-I get a pat, please?"* This is a more socially acceptable action-prompting behavior and it should be reinforced.

Examples of Action-Prompting Behaviors

Situation	Dog's Behavior	Owner's Response	Dog's Reward
1	Dog paces floor, whines, and barks in early morning hours, which annoys his sleeping owner. "Yo, dude! Wake up, I'm hungry!"	Talks to dog—possibly scolds (still attention for the dog)—lets dog outside, and feeds dog breakfast.	Attention from mom, chance to relieve himself, and then breakfast—what a life!
2	Dog is in back yard barking and bouncing on and off owner. "Yo, dude! Play with me!"	Finds a tennis ball and throws it for her hyper dog in hopes of "burning off a little steam."	The joy of barking, attention from mom, followed with an exhilarating game of ball retrieve.
3	Owner is sitting down. Dog sticks nose under owner's arm and repeatedly flips her hand up in air. "Yo, dude! Pat me!"	Owner pats dog and then asks dog to go and lie down.	First gets mom's attention and then gets pats on demand.
4	Dog is barking and bouncing off door as owner attempts to let him outside. "Yo, dude! Get that door open!"	Possibly scolds dog (attention) followed by letting dog, who has misbehaved, go outside.	Again the joy of barking and attention from mom, plus the fun continues by the chance to run and play outside.

Your dog routinely displays action-prompting behaviors. You need to become more observant at recognizing them so that you can distinguish between the *"mother-may-I"* that is pleasing to you and should be rewarded, and the less-attractive *"yo, dude"* that needs to be extinguished. The table below outlines four situations where an owner has reinforced an undesired *"yo, dude"* from his or her dog. By altering their responses, owners can stop reinforcing unwanted behaviors in their dogs and can encourage more favorable *"mother-may-I"* responses.

It is not that our dogs are masterminds of manipulation, nor are they plotting to get us to act on all their wishes. The truth is that our dogs' action-prompting behaviors are repeated due to a history of reinforcement. You can now turn this around and reinforce more appropriate responses as outlined in the table.

More Suitable Owner Response	New Lessons for the Dog
If dog wakes you up, potty him on leash without any interaction and go back to bed. If he disturbs you once more, he goes into his crate until you decide to get up. Any morning you wake up and your dog is sleeping in his bed be lavish in your attention to him.	Don't bother mom when she is sleeping unless you really have to pee. Staying in your own bed is a good thing.
Turn your back or attend to something else in the yard while ignoring dog. If necessary, put dog in house without you. Times when dog is quiet in yard, bring out the ball before he starts to act up.	Barking and bouncing eliminates the possibility of a game. Acting quietly is a way to initiate a game.
Ignore nose flip or leave room or crate dog. Pat and praise dog when he lies near you but before he performs nose flip behavior.	Don't bother mom when she is sitting down. Lying quietly is a good thing.
Wait until dog sits, reward with cookie, and then open door. If dog doesn't sit, walk away from door or crate dog.	Reckless behavior at the door causes it not to open. If I want to go outside I need to first sit quietly.

It is time for you to identify and make a list of your own dog's favorite action-prompting behaviors. Decide which of these responses are ones you would like to keep in your dog's repertoire and which need to be eliminated. Once you are aware of what your dog is expecting, you will be able to respond promptly and appropriately. If your dog gets a response from you that does not reinforce his behavior, he will be less likely to try the behavior again.

The more rewarding a *"yo, dude"* behavior has been for the dog, the more reinforcement you will need for the alternative, more desirable *"mother-may-I"* behavior to develop in its place. Consistency is the key to success. Every time your dog gives you an undesirable *"yo, dude,"* you must ignore him, leave the room, put him in his crate, or respond in a way that produces the opposite result to what your dog is demanding. When your dog gives you a more appropriate *"mother-may-I"* behavior, be certain to reward him to increase the probability that it will be repeated in the future.

Note: If your dog's behavior is self-reinforcing (for example, chewing on the furniture or barking at the cat), you cannot just ignore it, since the reinforcement is likely to continue when you leave. In this case, you need to remove the dog from the environment.

Nothing Is Free

Ask for a "control" behavior (such as a sit, down, or hand-touch) prior to offering your dog a privilege. Nothing he values comes free anymore. Your dog must earn all of the rewards you give to him.

Before you open his crate door to let him out, your dog must sit or lie down.
Put your hand on the crate door and ask your dog for a sit (or a down). Once he sits, praise him and open the crate door; if he stands up, close the door and stand up. Put your hand on the door and ask for a sit again. Repeat this process until your dog will sit with the door open, then give him a treat, attach his leash, and release

him. Be sure *you* are the one making the decision to release him from his crate. Once he is out of the crate, ask for another sit and praise and treat him again. Every time your dog comes out of his crate, you want him to greet you, rather than running to see what the other dogs are doing.

 Many dogs *"yo, dude"* their owners when the crate door is opening and bolt out past them. Not only is this another case of stealing reinforcement, it is potentially dangerous. If your dog bolts from a crate located in the back of your van, he could be injured, not only from the fall, but possibly by a passing car. You need this control in order to ensure his safety and also to allow him to earn the privilege of leaving his crate. Work for a more appropriate response from your dog, such as "look at me sitting at my crate door, *mother-may-I* come out?"

Before you open an outside door, your dog must sit or lie down. Repeat the procedure for releasing the dog from his crate for doors to the outside in your home. Soon, the stimulus for the dog to sit should be you putting your hand on the doorknob or the crate door, since it is always followed by a cue to sit. Your dog will be on-leash and wearing a head halter when at the door to go outside, so you will be able to prevent him from bolting out the door. He needs to hold the sit with the door open until you release him to go outside. Be certain to use food rewards to help your dog choose to sit each time you are near the door.

Before he is allowed to eat, your dog must do a sit-stay or down-stay while you put his food dish down on the other side of the room and then call him to a sit in front of you. Initially, this may need to be done with your dog very close to you and on a lead and halter so you can help him to be successful. You will be hand feeding most of his dinner, but you can leave a few kibbles to teach him control before the dinner dish goes down. Work toward having him sit further away from you as well as your moving before you release him to his dinner dish.

To initiate fun, your dog must touch your hand with his nose. Suppose the fun your dog wants is a game of fetch. Prior to every throw, have your dog touch your hand with his nose (in the beginning attach a long line to his regular collar so that you can control the game). Use the nose touch to initiate any game or any fun thing that your dog wants. If you have not taught a nose touch to your dog, see "Hand Targeting" later in this chapter.

Before getting a treat, your dog must do at least one behavior. No more freebies! All treats are given as rewards for a job well done. Do not have treats visible, or even reach for the cookie jar, before your dog has done what you have asked. Treats are *rewards* given *after* a job has been performed correctly, not bribes to get the job started. You may ask for a behavior as simple as a sit or getting into the crate. Regardless of what cue you have given, do not present the reward until the dog performs the behavior correctly.

Positive Is Not Permissive

Always maintain criteria for the behaviors you expect of your dog. Ask only *once* for a behavior and then be sure you control the consequence of that behavior. It may be a pleasurable consequence, such as a reward, or an undesirable consequence, such as a time-out.

Relationship-Building Games and Management Tools

During the various stages of the Ruff Love program, there are games the two of you can play together that will enhance your relationship. Through these games, you can convey to your dog that work and play are one and the same. Your dog's attitude about his work will improve as you get more control and focus from him.

Do not be limited by the suggestions included here. Use your imagination to create more games that encourage your dog to look to you as his source of fun.

When playing games with your dog, always keep the following rules in mind:

- Be sure that *you* are always having fun. Your dog can tell if you are just "going through the motions" of the game. Energy begets energy, so be exciting to your dog.

- Only use rewards that your dog *really* likes. For example, if your dog is not keen on toys, do not try to use them as a reward during these games. You must shape your dog's drive for toys *before* you can use them as reinforcement.

- Be certain that *you* start and end all games. Once your dog decides that he really likes a game, he may try a *"yo, dude"* to initiate play. If work equals play, then you need to establish rules that your dog must follow during both play and work. If you demand respect from him during your games, you are more likely to get his focus during your other training sessions.

- Never ask your dog to play and then let him decide he would rather not play. If you try to engage him in a game, the start of the game must be so rewarding that he would never turn you down. If he is too distracted to play, you must move to a less stimulating environment.

- Keep your play sessions very brief; if you play too long, your dog may get tired and end the game himself. If this happens, be sure to document in your journal the length of play time that is optimal for your dog at his current level of training. This will allow you to keep "shut down" from happening again.

Gimme Dat Collar

There may be times when you will have to lunge for your dog in haste; for example, to get him away from danger. The Gimme Dat Collar game teaches your dog that touching his collar is a good thing and that even your grabbing his collar is not something of which to be afraid.

Start by having treats your dog really likes. Reach down and touch your dog's collar and then give him a treat. The collar touch will soon become like a "click," telling your dog that good things happen when you touch his collar. Gradually start to grab the collar, faster and faster, before you reward your dog. Eventually, your dog will offer you his neck when he sees you lower your hand.

You can take this game one step further by holding the food treat in your mouth so that after you grab his collar, you reach toward your mouth for your dog's reward. This encourages your dog to look up at your face when you touch his collar. If your dog looks at you when you touch his collar, he is less likely to be distracted by other stimuli in his environment.

Hand Targeting

If you have not taught your dog to touch his nose to your hand, this is a great relationship-building skill you can work on. You can use hand targets to redirect your dog's focus away from a distraction or to get your dog into position beside you. Once learned, hand targets are also a good way to raise your dog's reinforcement rate for a training session: Hand targets present little challenge to most dogs, therefore it is easy for them to be successful.

Put a cookie in your hand, close your fist around it, and lower it to your side. When you dog comes to investigate, say "yes" or click and then open your hand so that he can get the cookie. Do this with your other hand as well. After two repetitions with each hand, lower your hand with your palm facing your dog. When he comes to investigate, say "yes" or click and retrieve a cookie from his dish (on a table beside you). Your dog will quickly learn that if he "bops" you in the hand with his nose, he can earn a cookie.

Once your dog knows this skill, you can lower your hand to get your dog to come close to you anytime you need his attention. You can also use the hand target as a control behavior that your dog must perform prior to getting a reward. Additionally, you can ask for a hand touch to initiate your dog's favorite game.

Note: To help lay down a great foundation for future dog sports, be sure that when you lower your hand to your side, it is slightly behind your hip when your dog comes in to touch it. The reason for this is because when you are moving in sporting events, it is better to have your dog at your side, rather than out in front of you.

1-2-3 Game

Through playing the 1-2-3 Game, your dog learns that he controls the reward as long as he plays by your rules—in order to get what he wants, the dog must first do what you want. This is called the **Premack Principle** of learning. The game transfers the enthusiasm your dog has for his favorite reinforcement into a game that eventually becomes just as reinforcing. The 1-2-3 Game intensifies the game of tug and teaches:

- Strong drive to an unmotivated dog.
- A quick sit or down to a driven dog.
- Focus toward the handler.
- An explosive release from sit and down positions.

Teaching the game consists of progressing through six stages. Work through these stages in very short sessions to maintain your dog's enthusiasm. Each repetition in any stage can last from one to ten seconds. Each session should not be any longer than two to three minutes in length. There is no minimum time to train; short training sessions are always good for motivation. Be sure to stop a training session while your dog's desire for the game is still very high. If you end when your dog's focus and drive starts to wane, you are teaching your dog to initiate "shut down" behavior. Remember, work equals play. You must always be the one who decides when work/play starts and ends.

Stage 1: Sit-Run-Tug

Start with a highly-valued toy. (If your dog isn't toy motivated, you can use a favorite food treat; you'll just deliver a treat to the dog instead of tugging.) Stand in front of your dog with one hip facing your dog so that you are perpendicular (at a 90-degree angle) to your dog. (As you play the game, vary standing with the dog on your left or your right.) Place the toy in the hand farthest from your dog and out of his sight. If at any point the dog looks away from you, do *not* continue. Wait until the dog chooses to look at you before continuing. Do *not* call or coax your dog to look at you.

Ask your dog for a sit or down. (Which one doesn't matter, but you will use the selected position until your dog has learned the entire 1-2-3 Game; only then can you try the game with another starting position.) Click the instant the dog's butt hits the ground and say "tug" or "get it," then turn and run away from the dog. This reaction should be *immediate:* click, then turn and run. When the dog catches you, present the reward in the arm furthest away from the dog so that the dog is always "driving" to the reward. The whole process should be very "snappy." Once you have delivered the reward, play with the dog to extend his reinforcement time, then ask your dog to drop the toy. (Initially, you may hold a cookie on the end of his nose to get him to drop the toy. However, if he continues in his reluctance to give up the toy, use the time-out method described on page 42.) Once the dog drops the toy, ask for another sit, then click and run away.

When you have achieved a success rate of 80% at this stage of the game, and your dog is very motivated when playing it, you can move on to Stage Two.

Note: It is important to have a cue (such as "tug" or "get it") which gives the dog permission to tug on the toy. Use your cue each time you initiate a game of tug. Don't make your dog guess when it is acceptable to tug and when it is not.

Stage Two: Learning Patience

Start perpendicular to the dog. Ask him to sit. Take one step sideways away from the dog so that you are adding a little distance between you and your dog. It is likely that the dog will want to come with you. (Don't get angry, this is a good thing!) Each time your dog's butt starts to lift up from the ground, return to him and ask him to "sit" once again. Be sure that you do not change the soft, friendly inflection in your voice when you repeat the cue "sit." There is no need to add a "stay" or "wait" cue; you are teaching the dog that "sit" means "sit until I give you something else to do." Continue to try to move one step away from your dog. Be patient and allow him to make the mistake of trying to follow you, since this means that your dog enjoys the game and can't wait for it to begin. Eventually, he will stop trying to move when you move away; that is when your game can begin. When he finally stays, click and say "tug," then run away and present the reward as in Stage One.

Your dog is experiencing the effect of the Premack Principle: In order for him to get what he wants, he first must choose to do what you want. You are teaching your dog that what you want him to do is exactly the same thing that he really wants to do!

Stage Three: More Patience

Step away and wait as in Stage Two, but delay the click for approximately two seconds. Click and run away and play. If you have success, you can now start to move several steps away (still perpendicular to your dog). Each time your dog waits in his sit, you will click and run away.

During this stage, be sure to alter the direction in which you are standing each time so that your dog sees both your right and left shoulder as a starting position. Also vary the number of steps you take away from the dog. The maximum distance you can be from your dog is dependent upon the drive and focus your dog has for the game. If your dog is glancing away or becoming disinterested, stay closer to him until you build more motivation for the game.

Stage Four: "Game-On" Body Position

In this stage, you will introduce the "game-on" position. This position will be a cue to your dog that you are about to start one of his favorite games. Move away from your dog and bend slightly at the knees as if you are ready to sprint away from him. You will still be standing perpendicular to your dog as you adopt this new game-on body crouch. Stare intensely at your dog as if you are daring him to try to catch you. Wait approximately two seconds before you click, say "tug," and run away. If your dog moves during any part of this process, return to the "game-off" body position, which is standing straight up. You can quickly move between the game-on and game-off position if your dog turns his head away, starts to sniff, or shows any other undesirable behavior.

Stage Five: Adding Motivational Breathing

In Stage Five, you will be building anticipation in your dog. You want him to make a mistake (as long as it is not more then 20-30% of the time.) By your dog anticipating the start of this fun game, he is telling you that he is keen to play. A dog who is driven to work with you is never bad; embrace his enthusiasm and remain patient.

Ask your dog to sit and move out into your game-on position. Now quickly inhale a breath of air very loudly. You can also "hype up" your dog by staring at him for a moment or taking one more step away before you start the game. Vary what you do so that you become more unpredictable, and therefore, more interesting to your dog. Occasionally click, say "tug," and run away as soon as you adopt your game-on position.

Stage Six: Backchaining Your 1-2-3

When your dog is very motivated to play the game, yet having success at Stage Five, it is time to add your motivational "1-2-3" phrase. In order to help your dog be successful, you will backchain this phrase. When you **backchain**, you train the last thing first so that you're training is always moving toward what your dog knows best. In this case, you'll teach the word "three" first, since it's the last element of the "1-2-3" phrase.

Get into your game-on position and say a drawn out "th-r-e-e-e-e-e." As this is the first thing you have ever said during the game, except for the word "tug," your dog will almost certainly get up. Remember to stay playful! Move out of the game-on position and wait until the dog sits (or return to him and tell him to sit). When your dog can stay while you say "th-r-e-e-e-e," tell him "tug," click, and run away to initiate a play session.

When you have had success with "three," you can add the word "two" before three (that is the concept of backchaining). You will move into position, say "t-w-o-o-o-o, th-r-e-e-e-e, tug!" and run away. Eventually, add the word "one" to give you the complete 1-2-3 Game!

Stage Seven: Using Lesser Rewards

When the game itself becomes rewarding because of what it represents, you can start using lesser rewards. This will help to build drive in your dog for other toys. However, the schedule of reinforcement remains continuous, meaning that your dog should always get a reward at the end of the game.

Sit–Tug–Sit Game

Break up any tugging session with frequent requests for a control behavior, such as a sit or down. A typical session should go something like this: sit–tug–sit–tug–lie down–tug–sit–lie down–tug, etc. You are trying to create a desirable *"mother-may-I"* response in your dog while playing this game. Once you ask for an "out" and your dog gives up the toy, ask for a sit or down; eventually, he will begin offering a sit or down when you ask for the "out." This is a desired *"mother-may-I"* response and should be reinforced. You can click, or say "yes," and then start the tug session again.

If the Dog Tries to Grab the Toy From You

If when you take the toy from your dog, he jumps up to grab it from you—"*Yo, dude, let's keep playing!*"—you need to give him a time-out. Take hold of his collar, gently guide his neck toward your leg and then hold his collar against your leg. Give the slack of the tug toy to the dog so that he can no longer tug (you have his collar so he cannot move and get any tension on the toy). Stand still and do not make eye contact with the dog. Do not pull on the toy; you are giving him a time-out for his inappropriate *"yo, dude"* behavior. Remember, the toy is yours; he can only play with it when *you* invite him to do so.

If the Dog Won't Release the Toy

The type of time-out described above is also effective for dogs that will not give up the tug toy on cue. Be patient and hold the dog's collar at your leg until he decides that playing the game this new way (you holding him and him not able to tug) is very boring. Once he drops the toy, click and reward with a treat. Occasionally click and reward with another game of tug.

Tug–Drop the Toy Game

This game is a good test of your progress with the Ruff Love program. With your dog on lead, initiate a game of tug. During your tug session, drop your end of the toy and back away from your dog, patting your leg to encourage him to follow you. If he comes back to you, praise wildly and continue the game of tug. If he runs off with the toy to play alone, quickly leave the room without speaking to him; close the door on the way out. If you have another dog in the house, get that dog and go back to the door. Have a tug session with your other dog on the opposite side of the door. After 90 seconds, go back into the room (without the second dog) and see what your Ruff Love dog does. If he jumps at you, praise, and then run toward the toy. If he runs to the toy and takes off with it again, repeat the above game with your other dog. If you don't have another dog, just go outside the door and whoop it up by yourself (draw the blinds first so the neighbors can't see you!). If after two chances, he still does not choose to come to you, take him by the leash and put him in his crate (without the tug toy).

At this stage, your dog still views playing with a toy by himself as more reinforcing than playing tug with you. It is unfair to continue to give him time-outs until you have further reinforced the game of tug *with* you. Continue to play tug games without surrendering the toy to your dog. Occasionally, after you have asked for an "out" and he has given up the toy, give him a high-value treat.

Hide & Seek Game

The Hide & Seek Game teaches your dog to watch you. Start by taking your dog to an area that is free of distractions and that is *secure, free of any possible escape outside.* (Rent an empty dog-training hall for 30 minutes if nothing else is available.)

Take your dog in and drop your leash. What are his choices?

- If he turns to look at you, pull out a toy and play wildly. Then spend the next five minutes trying to run away from him. Each time he catches you, reward him wildly. This is a huge step: *he is choosing to be with you!*

- If, on the other hand, he takes off running to investigate his new surroundings, run in the opposite direction and hide—do *not* say anything to indicate that you are leaving. You want to stay hidden until your dog starts to worry about you. If he starts to look for you but cannot find you, make a goofy noise (do not use his name). When he is really worried, look for a chance when he is not looking in your direction and then come out of hiding and run in the opposite direction from him, making a noise. When he chases you down, reward with his highest-level reinforcement. This will not be successful if there are reinforcement options for the dog in the environment, since he will not care where you have gone.

Remember that all behaviors have a consequence. With Hide & Seek you are teaching your dog that if he takes his eyes off you, you will not be there when he turns around. You are making your dog responsible for keeping track of your whereabouts, rather then letting him do what he wants and leaving you to chase after him when you want him to come back to you!

Teaching "Side" and "Close"

Teach the behaviors "side" (to come to your right side) and "close" (to fall into position on your left side). If your dog can take a walk and switch sides routinely when asked (either "side" or "close"), you will have a great management tool to use when walking near other dogs or distractions. Rather then gathering up a tight lead while walking by another dog, you can give the "side" cue to tell the dog to flip behind you so that he is walking next to you on your right side. If you cue the "close" behavior, he will flip to your left side and walk in heel position next to you. This action allows you to have your body between the strange dog and your dog.

By being proactive you will alter the situation so that your dog is less likely to feel the need to guard you or act aggressively toward oncoming dogs. This skill is also beneficial for the exuberant dog who loves to visit other dogs. It will give him a job to do before he has to pass by a potential new friend. Giving your dog a job to do when he sees another dog will make him less likely to get "charged up" around other dogs. This is also a great skill to take advantage of when you are walking your dog at a crowded dog show. Moving your dog away from strange dogs coming toward you prevents any possible interaction or potential altercation. This is of particular importance for small dogs, which can become a target for overly enthusiastic larger breeds.

Begin with your dog in a sit behind you. Say "side" and pat your right leg. Click the dog when he gets to your right side and deliver a cookie to him on that side. Repeat the process with your dog coming up to your left side when you say "close" and pat your left leg. Eventually you can stop patting your leg, as your dog will be responding just with the verbal cues. Remember to present the verbal cue *before* the physical cue. You can also add a sit at your side when your dog reaches either "side" or "close."

Chapter Five
Tracking Your Ruff Love Progress

Start a journal for your dog (see Appendix Two for a sample journal pages). On the first page, grade your current relationship with your dog on a scale of 1–10, with 1 being the lowest. This grade should be based upon:

- the status of your dog's recall.
- your dog's enthusiasm and drive to work with you.
- your dog's focus on you in the presence of distractions.
- your dog's history of looking for reinforcements from his environment rather than from you.

Revisit this page at the beginning of each month and create a new relationship "report card."

Making a List of Reinforcements
Reinforcements are things that *your dog* likes and that reinforce behaviors, making them more likely to be repeated. Start a section

in your journal for a list of reinforcements. Divide your list into three sections.

- First, list all of the possible **food** rewards that you can think of; do *not* limit the list to just the food rewards that you already know your dog likes.

- Next, list of all of the **toys** you think a dog might enjoy playing with; for example, squeaky toys, tennis balls, plush toys, and so on.

- Finally, list of all the **activities** that a dog might find reinforcing. Activities can be chasing a ball, going for a car ride, rolling in mud puddles, swimming, etc.

Remember that these are things that *a dog* might like and view as "true" rewards. They are not necessarily things that you like or even find acceptable.

If you are having trouble thinking of possible reinforcers, visit our website at www.clickerdogs.com. Select "Articles" from the home page and then "List of Reinforcers." This is a comprehensive list that can help you if you are stumped for ideas.

Ranking Reinforcements

Once your three lists are complete, rank the importance of these rewards to your dog within each one (food, toys, and activities):

- **"A" rewards** are those reinforcements that your dog will take any time, any place.

- **"B" rewards** are those reinforcements that work most of the time, but not all of the time.

- **"C" rewards** are those reinforcements that your dog will only take in certain, ideal conditions.

- **"D" rewards** are those reinforcements that your dog has only liked once in a while.

- **"E" rewards** are those reinforcements that your dog will *not* take any time or any place.

Food
Hamburgers – A
Popcorn – C
Cheese – B
Apples – D
Bacon – A
Milkbones – E
French fries – A
Ice cream – A
Peanut butter – B
Snausages – B
Ice cubes – B
Cat food – A

Toys
Frisbee – E
Tennis balls – B
Sticks – A
Snow balls – B
Kong – C
Soda bottles – A
Leashes – B
Sofa cushions – A
Bicycle tires – C
Socks – A

Activities
Chasing cats – A
Barking – A
Belly rub – C
Chasing his tail – D
Fence running – B
Chasing the vacuum – A
Tugging on you – B
Swimming – B
Cuddling – C
Hand targeting – C
Running in park – A

Identifying Behaviors to Eliminate and Rewards to Control

Remember the list of action-prompting behaviors that you made in Chapter Four. Make a list in your journal of the behaviors you would like to eliminate. Write a possible *"mother-may-I"* behavior to replace your dog's current *"yo, dude"* behavior. For example, suppose that your dog loves going for car rides and jumps up and scratches the passenger door before you can get him in the car. This is a *"yo, dude"* behavior that you want to change. A more acceptable *"mother-may-I"* behavior would be to have the dog run to the door, sit, and wait for you to let him in the car.

Check your list of reinforcers again. Your goal with your food and toy rewards is to turn the rewards you have ranked a "D" or an "E" into "A" rewards for your dog. If there are environmental rewards your dog is taking, make a note of those in your journal. All of the reinforcements your dog has been taking for himself need to be replaced with reinforcements that he earns from you.

Other Sections for Your Journal

In your journal, you also want to have a section for each of the following:

- **Recall progressions**—As you work on your recall daily (see Appendix One), you need to review and reevaluate your list of distractions. What was once a "4" distraction may now be only a "0" distraction. You also need to document where you worked on each recall.

- **Undesirable behaviors**—To affect a change in your dog's behavior you need to write down any unacceptable response your dog may display. This is particularly true if you are working with an aggressive dog or puppy. Document incidents of lip curling, growling, snapping, or even staring. Other "normal" behaviors such as stealing reinforcements, chasing the cat (why was he off leash?), or grabbing a toy from you should also be documented so you can work at altering these responses.

- **Training sessions**—This will be the main section of your journal. You should document all of your training sessions. Be sure to write dates, time of day, your mood, your dog's mood, treats used, toys used, what distractions were around, and any other information you feel may be of importance.

Why is it important to keep these records? Animal training great, Bob Bailey states that most training problems can be attributed to three things:

- **Criteria**—Are you clear in your mind what response you are waiting to see from your dog before you click and reinforce? You also need to be aware of what you *do not* want to reinforce. By keeping in mind any responses you would not like to see from your dog, you will be sure to ignore them should your dog offer one.

- **Timing**—Do you and your dog both agree on what you are clicking? If your click is consistently coming before or after the dog has performed correctly, he may not associate the click with the correct response. Have another trainer watch you to see if he or she can name the response that you are trying to select with your click. If this is not possible, videotape your training session and watch it yourself.

- **Rate of Reinforcement**—Is your rate of reinforcement too low? Be sure to document both the percentage of the time your dog experiences success as well as the number of times that he is incorrect (you should aim for 70-80% correct). Also document your dog's rate of response (see Chapter Three.)

By documenting everything you can, you will be able to see if there are **triggers** that cause unwanted behaviors to surface. You will also be able to identify any lack of progress in developing desired behaviors.

Well-kept journals are also very reinforcing for trainers, since you can look back on where you have come from and realize your hard work is paying off!

Chapter Six
Ruff Love for Puppies

If you are starting on the program with a young puppy (eight to ten weeks old), your goal should be to limit the puppy's privileges until he has learned what is acceptable and what is unacceptable behavior. The fundamentals of the Ruff Love program are the same for puppies as they are for older dogs. However, there are modifications you will make with your puppy's Ruff Love program.

You should not give your puppy freedom until he has been reinforced by you enough to choose correct responses. For example, you should not leave your puppy unsupervised in your living room while you prepare supper in the kitchen. By doing so, your puppy may "choose" to chew your furniture. You will have inadvertently rewarded his choice since you gave him the freedom to make the decision to chew. Chewing the furniture can be fun, and perhaps rewarding to the puppy, so he will likely try it again in the future. Scolding the puppy afterward will not alter the reinforcement value he has already received.

If your puppy is always supervised when he has free time, both inside and outside your home, you will be aware of what is rewarding him in his environment. Through your supervision you can encourage correct responses. In the previous example, the puppy under your supervision would be chewing a suitable bone or puppy chew and therefore would not get a chance to chew furniture. Raising a puppy in this manner allows a strong bond to develop between dog and owner since your relationship will be based solely on positively rewarding correct responses rather than intimidating your puppy and scolding him for "bad" behavior.

Look for and reward what you like in your puppy's actions. If you see undesirable behaviors remember your puppy is only a reflection of what you have taught him. Do not be disappointed or angry at your puppy; he can only be as "good" as you have raised him to be!

What Parts of the Book Do I Use With a Puppy?

Chapters Three, Four, and Five contain information that is applicable even if you are starting the program with a puppy. The Ruff Love for Puppies program requires the same level of commitment from you as a trainer as outlined in Chapter Three. You will also need to apply the program criteria from Chapter Four. Tracking your progress as described in Chapter Five may not be as necessary for a puppy that is being raised as a family pet, but it may be fun to look back on in the future. However, if you intend to train your puppy for competitive canine sports, it is beneficial to start your recordkeeping now.

You will start your puppy in Stage One of the program and will likely need to wait until you puppy is seven months of age before you move to Stage Two. Do not be in a hurry to progress too quickly through Stage One with your youngster, since he may not be mentally ready for more freedom. Puppies mature at different rates.

Ruff Love for Puppies follows the four stages outlined in Chapters Seven through Ten with the following special considerations:

- Your puppy will require more frequent trips out of his crate than an older dog because young puppies do not have complete bladder control.

- Keep your training sessions very short. Three to five minutes is the *maximum* amount of time you should work with a young puppy. It is better to train your puppy five to seven times during the day than to attempt fewer sessions of longer duration. Be sure to keep your reinforcement rate very high (80-100%), since your puppy is just learning all his new tasks.

- Shape your puppy's acceptance of the head halter. Although you may not need to use the halter for weeks, or perhaps months, you want to prepare your puppy right away for future use. Start by holding the nose loop open for your puppy to investigate. Click and reward any initiative towards the halter. Raise your criteria gradually. Your puppy will learn to enjoy seeing the halter since it represents desired rewards that are coming his way. Progress with this shaping process until your puppy will happily tolerate wearing his head halter.

- Try to enroll your puppy in puppy socialization classes. In these classes, your puppy will learn the proper way to interact with other puppies. While at class, be sure you control your puppy's free play with other puppies by requiring constant interaction with you. Once your puppy is brave enough to visit another puppy, allow the puppies to play only briefly (15-20 seconds) before you call your puppy back to you. Once he comes to you, reward him with a treat, ask him to sit, and then tell him to *"go and play."*

By interacting with your puppy and controlling these play sessions, you are once again reinforcing the concept that all fun things come from you.

- It is not necessary to crate your puppy away from other household pets when you are away from home. When you are home, it is a good idea to crate the puppy near you. During the puppy's first few nights in his new home, you can place his crate on a chair beside your bed. Allowing the puppy to see you will help him adjust to his new surroundings faster. Eventually you may choose to keep your puppy's crate in the room where you are working at any particular time. During Stage Two you can start to build confidence in your puppy by crating him away from you.

- Hand-feeding your puppy helps further develop a strong relationship between the two of you. However, your puppy also needs to learn how to eat a meal from his bowl. Be sure to let him eat part of a meal from his bowl, while alone, at least three times per week.

- The most important skill you can work on with your new puppy is your recall. Have someone restrain your puppy while you move away from him. Call your puppy and then run away. When your puppy catches you, reward him with a fun game of tug. Play this game as often as you can throughout the day and follow up with the recall exercises in Appendix One.

Ruff Love for puppies is *not* meant to be an isolation program. Be sure to get your puppy out of his crate for frequent training sessions throughout the day. Ideally, your puppy will be trained for one to five minute sessions as often as you can.

A typical training schedule might look like the this:

1. Wake up, take puppy outside, dish out puppy breakfast and add some attractive training treats to it. Training **session one** for puppy (you will likely not be able to finish all the kibbles in one session).

2. Take your puppy outside again (puppies often need to go to the bathroom after eating) then put him in his crate—you eat breakfast, shower, etc.

3. Training **session two** is prior to your leaving for work.

4. Training **session three** is at lunch (if possible).

5. Arrive home after work, let puppy out, prepare his supper and work through another brief training session (**session four**).

6. Let puppy out after his supper and then crate him in kitchen while you prepare your family's supper.

7. After supper have training **session five**.

8. Sometime in the evening let puppy socialize with you and family while you relax, then crate him for at least an hour (training **session six**, this one is less formal).

9. Training **session seven** happens one hour prior to your bedtime. This session will use toy/tug rewards rather then food rewards. You do not want to give puppy treats prior to your going to bed or you may be awakened during the night to let your puppy out. Puppy will need to drink after this session and you can let him outside just prior to your going to bed.

Chapter Seven
Stage One of Ruff Love: All Privileges Are Gone!

Ruff Love is not an isolation program. You want to continue to expose your dog to all of life's stimulations. The difference is that you will control the exposure. In Stage One of Ruff Love, your dog will hit "the wall" of change. All the good things that he has always had at his disposal will now be gone. This stage will likely last for at least seven weeks for all dogs.

The Crate

Your dog needs to spend most of his time in a crate. The crate should be placed in an environment where he will not be exposed to any other dogs in your home. Therefore, you may need to have two crates for him: one in your living environment that you can use when other dogs are not around and one outside of this environment where he can be when your other dogs have run of the house.

Each time you ask your dog to get in his crate, reward him with a favorite treat. During Ruff Love, you want to build up the motivational value of the crate; therefore, the dog is rewarded each and every time he is asked to go into his crate (unless he is going in there for a time-out). Be sure to use your treat as a reward and *not* as a bribe or lure. This means that you don't toss the treat in the crate or hold it out near the crate; you ask the dog to get in his crate and you present his reward after he is in the crate!

If your dog barks in his crate, someone (ideally *not* you) should cover his crate with a blanket so that he cannot look out from any side. After two minutes of silence, the cover should be removed. If you get into a routine of covering and uncovering his crate, he will soon learn the consequence of his behavior. If he continues to bark while covered, his crate will need to be moved to a more remote location so that his barking goes unnoticed until it is extinguished.

Your dog should stay in his crate unless you have time to supervise his activities. Take him out of the crate only on leash. If you want to spend one-on-one time with him, he should be on leash. For example, if you want to watch TV with him, give him a bone and ask him to lie at your feet while on leash. (Ideally, you will do some training to let your dog work his mind and body prior to your asking him to lie still while he's outside the crate.) He should also be on leash while working (unless your recall is 99.9% effective in all situations). All other dogs in your home should be put in another part of the house whenever your Ruff Love dog is having his time out of the crate.

As you progress through Stage One, your dog can be in his crate with the door open, provided he will stay in there and chew on his bone while you are watching TV or doing computer work, etc.

The Head Halter

A **head halter**, such as the Gentle Leader®, is a control tool, similar to a leash or any other type of collar. It gives you more control over your dog's behavior than any other humane aid available to you.

As with any training aid, your goal when you use a head halter is to train your dog so well that you no longer require its assistance.

It is important that the halter be properly fitted to your dog per the manufacturer's recommendations (snugly enough that your dog cannot paw it off when left alone). If you have a breed of dog with sensitive skin, purchase some moleskin (usually available in the foot section of pharmacies) to wrap around the nose loop of the halter so that it does not irritate the dog. You may also need to tape up the lead attachment that hangs beneath the dog's chin to prevent his chewing on it or trying to play with it.

For the first three days of the program, keep the head halter on 24 hours a day—even when the dog is in his crate. After this initial three-day adjustment period, you can start to remove the halter at bedtime when you put the dog in his crate. In order for the dog to be released from his crate in the morning, he needs to put his nose through the halter nosepiece. If he tries to bolt past you—*"Yo, dude. I don't need no stinkin' halter!"*—close the door and try again later. Once he allows you to put the halter on, reward him with a treat and then snap on the leash to take him outside.

Your dog will wear his halter whenever he is out of the crate throughout this stage of the program.

There may come a point in the program when your dog decides "to get out of this crate I need that halter on... so I am just going to sit here at the back of the crate and not go out." Here is where a little competition can help you. Get another dog (yours or a friend's) and play with that dog in front of the Ruff Love dog's crate or feed him in front of the Ruff Love dog's crate. Put the other dog away and then open the Ruff Love dog's crate and present him with a second opportunity to come out, if he accepts his halter.

It is human nature to be anthropomorphic about the head halter. You may think, "ahhhhh he looks so depressed" or "he isn't his happy self when his halter is on." Many horses don't like their first few days in a halter. However, once they get used to wearing one, they hardly realize it is there. If you use the halter intermittently, the dog will realize that the boundaries of control you are trying to establish only need to be observed when the halter is on. Also, if you take the halter off whenever your dog gives you his best depressed, sad puppy look (like the dog in the photo above), you will reinforce this behavior, causing him to continue to offer you the same sad response every time you put on the head halter.

Using Your Head Halter

When you take your dog out for training for the first time with his new head gear, have lots of treats on hand and, of course, your clicker. Encourage him to play a game like hand touching to get his mind off the halter. Try to keep a "J" shape in the lead so it isn't taut. Do not, at any time, "pop" the lead when a dog is wearing a halter. You want to avoid correcting your dog for any reason, but this is especially true if he is wearing a head halter since there is potential for damage to his neck.

If you want to redirect your dog's attention, grasp the lead near the clasp and hold your dog's head high and tilted back toward you. Avoid letting the dog get his head between his legs or rub his face along the ground or on his paws. Although he may be trying to rub the halter off or scratch his face, this behavior is reinforcing for him and will interfere with a consistent training session. If he puts his paw over the lead, let him figure out how to take it off—if you keep removing it for him, this will become a form of avoidance and will allow him to continue to gain attention. If he struggles, say nothing; just pull up until he first relaxes, then release the halter tension, and click and reward.

Give lots of verbal praise and frequent rewards while he is walking nicely beside you. As he learns not to pull on the leash, you can give this informal walking position a command, such as "with me." This is different than your command "heel," since all it asks of the dog is to walk nicely beside you without pulling.

Do not be discouraged if your dog "fights" the new halter. Remember back to when he was an eight-week-old puppy: he pulled, scratched, and didn't like his regular collar. Many dogs adjust to the head halter very quickly, but if yours doesn't, you need to persevere. Remember, if you ever take a halter off your dog because you think he looks uncomfortable, you will be rewarding your dog for looking uncomfortable, and you can count on that behavior returning—all behaviors have a consequence!

Working With the Halter in a Distracting Environment

If your dog's focus is drawn away from his work, use the halter to help bring his attention back to his work. It is important not to speak to your dog when you are engaging the halter—even a reprimand is a form of reinforcement. Simply hold the dog's lead up and slightly behind you and wait him out. Once the dog relaxes, praise and feed. If your dog becomes excited while you are praising him, pull his head up and repeat the above process until his attention is *not* focused on the distraction, but rather totally on you. If he can maintain a relaxed state for a few seconds, click and reward him.

Anticipate when your dog is going to lunge at another dog or some other "target" by watching where he is looking and observing his body posture. Try to get his attention on you or on another task (such as hand targeting) before he lunges. Encourage your dog to engage in an incompatible behavior before he becomes too excited (for example, lying down or sitting, looking up at you, etc.) and remember to reinforce any appropriate behavior the dog offers.

If you ever find yourself cooing the phrase "that's okay" in this type of situation, stop immediately: you are actually reinforcing whatever your dog is doing at the time, and chances are, he is behaving in an inappropriate way.

"Potty" Retraining

Your dog should go out to potty on a leash or long line. If you are competing in obedience, flyball, or agility away from home, your dog will have to eliminate at your hotel while on leash, so this is a good time to teach him. Be sure to take out your dog by himself. At first, you may need to use a long line rather than a leash, since the dog may not be used to doing his "business" with you close by. Give him three minutes to eliminate. If he hasn't performed by then, take him back to his crate. Try again in 30 minutes. By limiting his time outside to eliminate, you are encouraging him to eliminate more quickly. You can gradually lower his allotted time until your dog wants to do his business as soon as he gets outside!

Supervised Socialization

In order to promote sound socializing skills it is important to allow interaction with other dogs in your household. However, because dogs often bond to other dogs faster then they bond with people, your dog's socializing during Stage One should be done only when there's also interaction with you. Your dog should not be allowed to have unsupervised interaction with other household dogs at any time. This includes going out to potty, which he should do *on leash* or on a long line and without other dogs.

- When you decide to allow a brief period of interaction, it should be with only one dog at a time and under your complete supervision.

- During his allotted time of brief interaction with one other household dog, call your Ruff Love dog over and reward him with a tidbit for coming away from the other dog. At first, you may need to put the treat right on his nose to get him away from the other dog.

- If your dog has dog-aggression issues or is more attached to your other dogs then he is to you, he should not be crated with or near another dog at any time during the next four weeks.

- While traveling in your car, use a blanket to cover his crate so he cannot see other dogs while traveling.

- If you are dealing with an aggression issue between two dogs in the household, do not allow any interaction unless both dogs are leashed. When rewarding one dog for appropriate behavior in the presence of the other dog, use verbal or physical rewards that are low enough in reinforcement value that your Ruff Love dog will not feel the need to guard. To further prevent against guarding, do not have any food rewards on your body; instead, hide them in high places around the room so that he cannot predict where they are coming from.

Hand Feeding

All of your dog's meals should be hand fed. If time constraints make this a problem, you need to change your current feeding schedule. For example, you may decide not to feed two equal-sized meals a day, but rather a small meal in the morning, when your time is short, and a larger meal in the evening, when you have more time. You can use his meal portions as rewards during a training session or you can feed him a handful at a time (be aware of *"yo, dude"* behavior creeping in here, such as pawing at your leg or jumping on you). By hand feeding your dog, you are reminding him how important you are to him and that all good things come from you.

By the end of Stage One, you can add more food to his bowl and use less to hand feed, if you wish. Continue to hand feed at least one of his meals each day. Many of us use meals to train our dogs long after we have finished the Ruff Love program. Our dogs never get a full meal in their bowl on a day we are training them.

No Toys

Your dog should have no access to toys except when interacting with you. For those of you with a large, over-stuffed toy box in your family room, pick it up and put it away so that you control when your dog is rewarded. By not having toys freely available to your dog, you are reinforcing the idea that all fun things come from you. The only time your dog sees toys is when you are training or playing a game with him (which, of course, you control by asking for sits and downs).

However, it is important that chew bones be made available to your dog at all times, both in and out of the crate. Rubber toys (such as a Kong or Havaball) stuffed with peanut butter and kibble may also be made available to him in his crate to help prevent anxiety behaviors from developing.

On Leash

Your dog should be kept on leash or on a long line any time he is outside. He is not allowed to run or swim with a group of dogs as you want to avoid a "pack mentality" from developing. However, he may be given access to these activities when alone with you—remember, your goal is for the dog to see you as the sole provider of all things worthwhile. When you allow your dog to run or swim, it should be with constant interaction from you. If he's swimming, call him out of the water and reward him with a game of tug or a treat. After you have reinforced him for coming to you, ask him to sit, lie down, or touch your hand. Once he is under your control, invite him to once again "go for a swim." You want the game of running to you to be as rewarding as the game of swimming or running. Activities like these need to be done on a long line during Stage One until the dog understands that even when he is swimming or running, he needs to come when he is called.

These restrictions may mean your dog gets less physical activity than usual, but this will be far outweighed by the mental and emotional benefits gained over the next six months. If you take the long line off before your dog is ready and he decides *not* to come out of the water when you call, you must be prepared to go in after him, *clothes and all!*

Relationship-Building Games and Management Tools

During Stage One, you will work with your dog on hand targeting, the Gimme Dat Collar game, and the Sit-Tug-Sit game. You will also start training "side" and "close" commands. Each of these is explained in detail in Chapter Four.

Special Training

Start some special training with your dog. Consider agility to build confidence, or formal obedience skill training, or tracking. Every new activity you engage in with your dog reinforces the concept that all activities worth doing involve interaction with you. Each time your dog has a positive training experience in a new location, he will become more capable of generalizing good behavior to other locations. Your dog will be learning to give you focused attention regardless of the environment in which you are training.

Recordkeeping

Remember to document your daily training sessions in your journal, making sure to include:

- Date, time of day, your mood, dog's attitude, what you have altered in your dog's daily routine, what your dog's response was to a new freedom you introduced

- Any new out-of-the-ordinary responses (such as your dog seeking eye contact from you when around a distraction)

- Your success rate and rate of reinforcement statistics

- New skills you are building and criteria selection

- Any general comments outlining what was good and what you want to work on during your next session

- Make a plan for your next training session

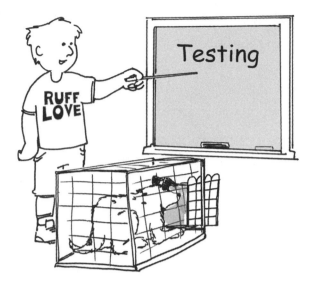

Chapter Eight

Stage Two of Ruff Love: Testing Your Progress

Stage Two may begin anywhere from six weeks to six months into the program, depending upon your success at Stage One. Before advancing to Stage Two, you must reevaluate your relationship with your dog. If you grade your relationship at least 50% higher than it was at the beginning of Stage One (check your journal), it is time to move ahead. For example, if you graded the relationship between you and your dog as a "2" when you started the Ruff Love program, do not progress to Stage Two until your relationship is graded at least a "4."

Stage Two is a testing stage where you determine if your dog will *choose* to do what you want him to do. You are, in effect, loosening up the restrictions you have placed on him to evaluate his reactions to more freedom. As you monitor his progress on a daily basis, don't be afraid to "pull in the reins" if your dog starts to revert to previous unwanted behaviors.

Adding Back Privileges to Test Your Dog's Reactions

Gradually, increase the number of privileges your dog can enjoy. Be sure not to add all the freedoms back at one time!

Crate Freedom

The crate is now left open most of the time. Your dog may go in, or not, whenever you are together. You may continue to reward him whenever you *ask* him to go in his crate and close the door. He will still be crated when you are not at home and at night.

Halter Freedom

You can now attach your lead to a regular collar (worn in addition to his head halter). It is important that your dog still wear his halter whenever he is out of his crate so that if you need it, it is available. Test your dog's leash respect by allowing him to walk on a regular collar in low-level distraction areas. Over the course of Stage Two, you want to gradually give your dog more opportunities to show you he can control himself in distracting environments. You need the odd failure to show you where the boundaries of his knowledge and understanding lie. During this transition stage, you may choose to attach one leash to his regular collar and one to his head halter. The halter lead should only be engaged if your dog's response on his regular collar is undesirable.

Remember, your goal with a halter is to get rid of it, so make sure that you are always using it as a learning tool and not as a crutch. You should be teaching your dog something when you engage the halter. Give your dog the opportunity to be correct without your holding his head up and controlling him throughout all distractions. If he is unable to control himself without your help, take him further away from the distraction and try again.

Socialization with Other Dogs

Provided he will come to you whenever other dogs are around, you can start to allow the Stage Two Ruff Love dog to socialize with dogs outside the household. Start by allowing socialization with a dog that will ignore your Ruff Love dog. While the dogs are interacting, call your Ruff Love dog away from the other dog and play a game of tug. It is not a bad thing if these dogs want to play with each other, but the Ruff Love dog must come out of play whenever you call him. If your dog will not come away from the other dog, you will need to restrict access to other dogs until Stage Three.

Meals

Work up to feeding 75% of your dog's meals in his bowl by the end of Stage Two. Whenever you have time in your day for training, you can mix some of the dog kibble with your training treats. Continue to have your dog sit before you present his dinner dish.

Leash Freedom

Inside, you can "fade out" use of the leash by attaching a light, nylon line of the same length for a week or two. You need to evaluate your success with your recall before you remove the line entirely. If your dog always responds the first time you call him, you can start to leave the line off. If your dog does not come when called, even once, you need to refer back to the recall work in Appendix One. The goal is to decrease your dependence on the leash, but you need to monitor your success.

Outside, in a fenced-in area, you can have the dog drag a 15-foot light, nylon line (it may need to be 25 or 35 feet for large or fast dogs). Again, if your dog fails to respond to you the first time you call him, even once, you will need to keep the line on for a longer period of time. Keep reevaluating your recall and gradually, fade out the use of the light line as you have success working through distractions in different environments.

Toys

Toys are still absent from your dog's living area—toys are special and are only produced when playing with you.

Taking the Tug Test

Follow the instructions for playing the Tug-Drop the Toy Game in Chapter 4. This is a good test of your progress in the program. Ideally, your dog will choose to come to you after you drop the toy and back away. If he does not "choose" to come after two attempts, you need to work on your tug game for another month before you try this "test" again. Your goal is to have your dog like to tug with you more than he likes to play by himself.

Relationship-Building Games and Management Tools

During Stage Two, continue to work with your dog on hand targeting, the Gimme Dat Collar game, the Sit-Tug-Sit game, as well as "side" and "close." Introduce your dog to the Hide & Seek game and also the 1-2-3 Game. Each of these is explained in detail in Chapter Four.

Chapter Nine
Stage Three of Ruff Love: The Light

There is light at the end of the tunnel! Welcome to Stage Three. Your dog has proven that he looks to you as the source of all good things. Your relationship report card grade is at least 75% of where you would ultimately like it to be. You will continue to loosen restrictions on your dog.

Adding Back Privileges
Continue adding privileges back into your dog life as you see improvement in his behavior.

- Your dog may sleep loose in your bedroom (on a dog bed or in his crate with the door open).

- You may choose to decrease your dog's time in his crate. However, be sure to continue to reinforce him each time you ask him to get in his crate and close the door.

- Your dog's head halter should be on only when you are going to work in highly-distracting environments.

- You can advance to no leash for potties, except for one day a week (this will help to remind him to potty on leash while staying in hotels).

- Because he has proven that he will come away from playing with any dog when you call him, your dog may now have free time with all of your household pets.

- Your dog may run with other dogs outside if his recall is 99.9% accurate. Use the chance to "go for a run" as a reward to your dog, not something he chooses when he wants. Make sure to keep testing him by calling him away from play to interact with you.

- The toy box can come back, but only one toy may be added to it.

- Mix some of his kibble with training treats for training sessions and feed him the rest of his meals in his bowl.

- Your dog does not need a leash on in the house. Outside, use the light line only in distracting environments when you are not sure he will watch you.

Relationship-Building Games and Management Tools

Expand the Hide & Seek game to include many locations, such as large fenced-in yards, agility class (lots of equipment to hide behind), and any other environments you have available. The more environments you train in, the more the behavior of keeping his eyes on you will generalize to *all* environments. Continue working on the 1-2-3 game.

Monitoring Progress and Recordkeeping

Keep notes on your training sessions and behaviors during this stage. Be proactive. If you see any undesirable behavior starting to resurface, do not hesitate to send your dog back to Stage Two.

Chapter Ten
Stage Four of Ruff Love: Management for a Lifetime

Remember, "positive is not permissive" and "all behaviors have a consequence." If your dog makes a choice you do not like, it is up to you to control the consequences that follow. If he receives reinforcement for his choice, he is very likely to try it again at some point in his life. Your dog may react in unexpected ways to a stimulus he has not experienced before, but you now have the tools to work through any situation. You will manage the amount of stimulation to which your dog is exposed. In this way, you aid in his education and help to further develop the bond between you.

Managing your Ruff Love graduate means you must always be aware of what is rewarding to your dog. Review the reinforcement and action-prompting behaviors lists in your journal and make changes as your relationship grows. Be sure you continue to grade your relationship so that you may take pride in all of your hard work. Your dog may be allowed on certain pieces of furniture, but only when you invite him. Always ask him to sit first and then release him to come up and cuddle on the sofa. It's also fine if you have decided that the few months without dog hair on the sofa was not a bad thing and want to continue to keep all dogs in their own beds on the floor!

Make a commitment to continue to apply the essential elements of Ruff Love from Chapter Three. As you continue to reinforce appropriate behaviors in your dog, you will find yourself innately making the correct decisions as a dog trainer. Be sure to review your journal on occasion and take pride in your hard work, knowing your dog truly is a reflection of your effort and abilities.

Once you are at Stage Four, you will have a new relationship with your dog. You can now enjoy the benefits of your diligence by having a dog that understands boundaries. Regardless of whether you are raising your dog to be a family companion or you have aspirations to be the best in the world at your chosen canine sport, developing a strong bond with your dog is always time well invested. Congratulations.

Recommended Reading

- *On Talking Terms With Dogs: Calming Signals*
  by Turid Rugass

- *How Dogs Learn*
  by Mary Birch Ph.D. & Jon Bailey Ph.D.

- *Learning and Behavior*
  by Paul Chance

- *The Culture Clash*
  by Jean Donaldson

- *Dogs Are From Neptune*
  by Jean Donaldson

Chapter Eleven
Ruff Love Questions and Answers

What if I need to go away without the dog?
If you must go away for a weekend or longer, be sure your dog sitter will not allow your dog to think he is suddenly visiting doggy Club Med. If your dog "parties it up" when you are away, he will likely be less than thrilled when you show up to take him back to "boot camp." Therefore, be sure that your dog lives with some guidelines while you are away. You cannot expect the people who are looking after your dog to follow every Ruff Love rule, but you can ask that your dog be crated, not allowed on the furniture, and not allowed hours of free time romping with other dogs.

What if other family members don't comply with the program?
In the perfect world, all members of a household abide by the guidelines of the Ruff Love program during their interaction with your dog. You cannot always expect all members of your household to care as much about their relationship with your dog as you do, but you can ask that they not contradict what you are doing.

Getting freedom from family members when you are not around gives reinforcement to unwanted behaviors, which will make the program take longer. At the very least, you can ask that household members don't undermine what you are trying to achieve. Your family can participate with your tutelage. If they don't wait for a sit or follow through with good dog-training skills, it will not affect your relationship with the dog. Your dog will learn to abide by one set of criteria with you and another set with other family members. It is ideal if everyone is on the same page, but not mandatory.

How can I be sure it is time for my dog to move on to the next stage of Ruff Love?

You do not want to rush the progression of your dog through the program. It is detrimental to add privileges back before your dog has had adequate reinforcement from you for choosing appropriate behaviors. When in doubt, stay another week at your current stage. Likewise, you need to challenge your dog so that you can see if he will make the right choices. Do not delay in giving your dog more freedom if he is continually choosing good behavior.

This program seems restrictive for a puppy. I don't want to isolate my puppy from things he needs to be exposed to.

Traditionally, puppies are raised with too much freedom. The puppies are educated by being "scolded" when they act inappropriately. Ruff Love is not meant to be an isolation program where you hope the dog learns to appreciate what he has by restricting everything he enjoys. Rather, it is a program that allows you to manage what is reinforcing your dog. You build up the frequency of correct behavior through your good timing and reinforcement. The puppy will not routinely "get into trouble" since his freedom and opportunity for environmental reinforcement is restricted. This program is not only meant to educate the puppy to behave in a socially acceptable way, but to also educate owners to be good at acknowledging when their dogs are behaving well.

Appendix One
The Recall

Following is a strategic approach to help you shape a more reliable response each and every time you call your dog. You need to work on your recall daily.

Devising a Plan

- In your journal, make a list of situations, people, toys, places, other animals, food, objects, or odors that your dog finds distracting to the point of not listening to you. If you need ideas, see the list of "Distractions for Your Recall" which is under "Articles" on our website at www.clickerdogs.com.

- Rate these distractions on a scale of 1 to 10, with 10 being the most distracting to your dog.

- For the next week, make a point of having your dog on a leash or long line any time he is around a distraction that is rated "2" or greater.

- You need to avoid any level "10" distractions for the next two months. This means that you are not going to allow your dog the freedom to choose not to come to you when number "10" distractions are in his environment. This may mean keeping your dog on leash for the duration of the Ruff Love program or until you are confident in the reliability of his recall.

Laying a Solid Foundation

In order to have success with recalls, you must put in the work. Make a point of doing recalls with your dog every day for a minimum of three sessions per day, three to five minutes per session. Following are some guidelines to help you during these sessions:

- Choose a word that you want your dog to understand means "come to me." It may be "come," "here," "com'ere," "front," or anything else you choose. Try to pick a word to which you haven't already attached meaning. For example, do not choose "come" if you have used this word in the past and your dog has learned to ignore it.

- Do not use your dog's name before the cue "come." In two months, once he fully understands his new cue "come," adding his name will have even more impact. If you start by saying, "Duke come," your dog will hear that as one cue. We would like the dog to respond to "Duke" and "come" as two separate cues from you.

- Use different motivators to reward your dog when he comes to you. Your motivators may be toys, different types of food, or anything else your dog goes "gaga" over.

- Be sure treats and toys are being used as a reward and not as a bribe. Call the dog, click him for coming, and then present the reward. Do not hold the treat or toy like a lure in front of his nose as then you are teaching your dog to come to you only if he can see the toy or food first.

- In your three to five minute long training sessions, you should be able to get in 15 to 25 recalls. In your initial sessions, be sure there are no distractions around so that your dog will want to come to you. You may even have someone help you by restraining your dog. Walk a short distance away, call out your cue "come," and run backward. Your dog should chase you, click and reward.

- Always vary your body position. Sometimes, call your dog and when he starts to come, run away so that he can chase you. Sometimes, start to run away, but then stop and let him come to you while you are standing still. Occasionally, don't run at all. Be unpredictable.

- As the week progresses, add a few of the distractions that rate a "'1" on your distraction scale. Remember to call your dog only once. If your dog chooses the distraction over you, score 1 point for him, minus 20 for you. You will then need to execute at least 20 additional successful recalls before you can progress with your homework. By the end of the week, your dog should be doing a successful recall with distractions of "2" or lower.

- If your dog does not come with one cue at any time during the program, lower your criteria. You may need to reduce the level of the distractions, if you are working with distractions. You may need to move closer to your dog or get more attractive rewards.

- Progress up the distraction chart as your dog allows you to, but not too fast. You want to try to work your dog in the presence of his number "10" ranked distractions, but not until you have diligently done your homework of at least eight weeks of recalls. After eight weeks, you should have put in an average of 20 recalls per training session, three times per day, seven days per week. Over the two months of work, this means that you have done at least 3,360 successful recalls with your dog.

- If your dog has a long history of not coming when he is called, you may need to extend this recall program. It may be more difficult for you to work your way up your distraction list. Be patient and only move forward with success. Rather than eight weeks, your schedule may be 16 weeks or more. The program will work if you are methodical and do *not* let your dog have the freedom to ignore a recall at any time.

Perhaps you haven't thought of every possible distraction your dog may encounter, but if you have worked through as many distractions as you can think of, in as many different locations as are available to you, your dog will start to generalize his recall to all locations.

Reinforcing Recalls

Following through with daily reinforcements for coming will give you a solid foundation of shaping your dog to want to run to you, each and every time you call, regardless of what distractions are in his environment. The reinforcement you give your dog for coming to you can be as obvious as a treat or a toy, but it can also be praise or pats from you, a car ride, or any one of the activities that reinforce from the lists you made in Chapter Five.

Appendix Two
Keeping a Journal

In your Ruff Love journal (see Chapter Five), you should have a section for each list you are asked to create during the program (such as the list of reinforcements), a section that documents recall progression, one for undesirable behaviors, and a section that documents your training sessions. The first page of the journal is your relationship "report card." At the beginning of each month, you will grade your current relationship with your dog.

Relationship Grade

January 2nd – 2

February 4th – 4 (Duke now has the beginnings of a recall and is enthusiastic during training sessions. Hasn't tried to bolt out of his crate or out the door for 10 days. Still distracted when other dogs are nearby.)

Date: Jan 20th **Time of Day:** 7:00 a.m. **Training Session #:** 1

Location: Living room **Rewards Used:** Kibble, hot dogs

Skill Focus: Hand touches, sits and downs

# of Correct Clicks	# of Unclicked Responses	Comments
⌇⌇⌇⌇ ⌇⌇⌇⌇ ⌇⌇⌇⌇ ⌇⌇⌇⌇ ⌇⌇⌇⌇ ⌇⌇⌇⌇ ⌇⌇⌇⌇ ⌇⌇⌇⌇ ⌇⌇⌇⌇ ⌇⌇⌇	⌇⌇⌇⌇ ⌇⌇⌇⌇ ⌇⌇⌇⌇ ⌇⌇⌇⌇ ⌇⌇⌇⌇ ⌇⌇⌇⌇ ⌇ ⌇	Had Duke work for all his breakfast. He had trouble with touches on my right hand. Did not want to lie down, so I sat on floor. He went down, I gave him a big handful of kibble and ended session.

Total: 48 **Total:** 32 **Session Time:** 10 minutes

Rate of Reinforcement: 48/10 = 4.8 rewards/minute

Success Rate: 48/80 = 60%

Follow Up: Next time I train, I need to make my session shorter and get my Success rate and rate of reinforcement higher. Need to work happier downs.

Date: Jan 20th **Time of Day:** 8:30 a.m. **Training Session #:** 2

Location: Back yard **Rewards Used:** Tug toy, biscuits

Skill Focus: Eliminating on leash and recalls

# of Correct Clicks	# of Unclicked Responses	Comments
⌇ ⌇		Took Duke out on leash for his last exercise before going to work. He finally did his business and I gave him a big handful of biscuits. Did 2 restrained recalls and rewarded with tug..

Total: 2 **Total:** 0 **Session Time:** 90 seconds

Rate of Reinforcement: 2/1.5 or = 1.3 rewards/minute

Success Rate: 2/2 = 100%

Follow Up: Low rate of reinforcement due to fact I needed time to move away from Duke to do restrained recall. Noticed that Duke is starting to be less distracted.

Appendix Three
Ruff Love for Agressive Dogs and Puppies

Aggression in a dog or puppy is often a complex problem, which requires the observations and advice of a trained professional. There are many different "triggers" that can cause a dog to act aggressively. Your puppy may grow up to be a well-adjusted dog who gets along with dogs, people, and children throughout his life, but he is dependent upon you and your choices for him. Unfortunately, the reality is that there is also the potential for your dog to develop into a socially deviant dog who does not know how to properly interact with other dogs (and possibly children) coming into his space.

Aggressive dogs often guard food, toys, and family members. This resource-guarding can turn out to be a full-time, anxiety-filled occupation for a dog. Through no fault of your own, your dog may be receiving all the reinforcement he needs to perpetuate his fear and aggression from both you and his environment. What may have started as a fear reaction to dogs or children in his space has now transformed into an overt act of aggression to keep all that he fears far away. Your puppy needs clear direction from you in order to develop a more socially acceptable personality.

Many dogs that show aggression toward dogs or people will never be 100% trustworthy in similar situations throughout their lifetime. The key is not to ignore any early signs of aggression but to work hard to reduce the reactions of your dog. Counterconditioning your dog to the stimuli that trigger his behavior will also help him to reduce his fears. Following are some training suggestions that may help you. **However, if you are encountering repeated episodes of aggression, please seek out the help of a trained animal-behavior counselor.**

Lifestyle Changes

Any dog that acts aggressively should be a permanent resident of Stage One of Ruff Love until you can work through his issues. By restricting your dog's freedom, you will not allow any aggressive incidents to take you by surprise. Every chance your dog gets to rehearse his aggressive behavior reinforces this event for him, making it more likely to reoccur the next time his trigger is presented.

Your Reactions

Many times dogs act aggressively toward things that frighten them. The first sign is often seen when a dog or puppy "alarm barks" at a stimulus that scares them. This alarm bark differs from your dog's normal barking behavior. It is a high-pitched bark often accompanied by the hair over his shoulders and rump standing on end. Your dog may stand up on his toes to try and make himself appear bigger to the "monster" he perceives. This behavior warns you that your dog has an issue with this particular stimulus.

The first response of many owners is to pick up the dog or to tighten the dog's lead as they back away, allowing the dog to continue to bark and growl. Doing this adds fuel to the fire. Guard dogs are agitated to become more aggressive toward the "bad guys" by their handler pulling back on the collar, away from the stimulating victim. You should act very nonchalant. Yawning will often help calm your dog, so try yawning at your dog. Turn your dog's head toward you as you back away from the stimulus and treat this situation like any other distracting environment. When you see your dog relax, reward him for this more appropriate response. You can click and reward him the moment he acts calmer. Just as in any other highly distracting environment, you want to work on the periphery of the environment where your dog will feel more comfortable. Do not try to train your dog in the middle of a stressful atmosphere since your success will be minimal.

Working Through Fears

The following situations deal with aggression in puppies toward other dogs. For aggression toward people, many of the same principles apply. You do not want to force a dog to take a cookie from someone who scares him. Work on the periphery, and click and throw the treats in the direction of the person (but not so close that your dog is cautious when picking up his treat). You may choose to ask your dog for a simple behavior, such as a hand touch. You may need to retreat to a distance further away if your dog is still afraid of the person. If your dog is only afraid of children, work through this fear in an environment where you know the children and you can control their actions. Never take a dog that is afraid of children to a park where children may rush up to him. Likewise, do not take a dog that is aggressive toward other dogs to a "leash-free" park where you cannot control the actions of the other dogs.

What to Do When Dogs or People Walk Toward You

Dogs or people walking toward you is a good thing! This is a lesson you need to teach your dog. Have a bait bag with many different reinforcers in it. Cheerios, raisins, and carrots can be considered a low-level reward. Dog kibble can be slightly above that. Store-bought moist treats can be a little higher. At the top of the list will be steak, chicken, cheese, and other favorites. The closer the dogs (or people, if that is what frightens him) get to your dog, the better the treats get and the more rapidly they come. Soon, he will like to have anyone and anything come close so that he can earn the best and the most treats. You can then work on teaching him to sit while dogs or people walk past him.

What to Do When Dogs Are Close

You must always watch your dog's eyes. He should be allowed to glance at other dogs in his environment; this is normal and will increase his feeling of security. But you must not allow more than a glance at any time. Once he has had his one look, you need to determine whether immediate caution should be taken.

Situation One: Potentially Volatile Situation—Gently, but firmly, pull up on your head halter so that your dog's eyes focus on you. When his eyes are on you, praise, but don't feed. Release the pressure so that you give your dog a choice: to keep looking at you or to look back at the other dog. If your dog continues to watch you, click or praise and then feed. If he chooses to look back at the other dog, turn his head toward you again. During this whole process, you should be slowly backing away from the stimulus which upset your dog. Thus, if it takes three or four turns of the head away from the other dog (or distraction), you are gradually putting distance between it and your dog. This makes it easier for your dog to be successful with the "watching you" behavior.

Situation Two: Little to No Chance of Your Dog Reacting to Other Dog—This may happen with dogs he is comfortable around or it may happen as you follow up on this course for longer periods of time. If you feel comfortable, your dog will not be overly stimulated:

ask him for a hand touch so he targets the palm of your hand with his nose. *Be sure to only ask once.* If your dog is not successful when you ask once, you need to consider this a Situation One and turn his head toward you.

Situation Three: Fearful Situation—If your dog starts to alarm-bark in fear of an approaching dog or person, try the program outlined by Jean Donaldson. At the first sight of distraction, feed rapidly until the person or dog leaves. Your puppy will soon associate the sight of something that was once scary as something that causes great rewards to be produced.

Controlling Socialization

These "puppy parties" are best done outside of your property, where your dog will feel less protective and less confident. During these parties, you want to be continually rewarding your dog for looking at and away from other dogs or for adopting a relaxed body position. Other dogs will read this relaxed body posture as being nonthreatening and therefore will avert their eyes and lower their body postures in response. Try to arrange these meetings with dogs that your dog will not feel the need to be defensive around (initially, use only more subordinate dogs). The more positive meetings he has with other puppies and dogs, the more information you can give him about how he should be acting. This will help him to generalize a more positive greeting ritual to all dogs and puppies.

Should an altercation erupt, do not tense up and pull your dog away; this is a trigger for your dog to become more aggressive. Instead, use his head halter to tip his head up toward you and then praise him.

Once you have your dog's focus, try to relax the pressure on the head halter. If he remains focused on you, click and treat; if he looks back at the other dog, continue to tip his head and test his responses. During this process, you should be slowly retreating from the stimulus of the other dogs in the environment, but do so only while you have control of your dog's head. Your goal is to have your dog adopt a non-confrontational body posture when other dogs get in or near his space. Laugh out loud, yawn, drop treats on the floor, but try to remain calm when he "freaks out" and do not pick him up or tighten your leash in a defensive mechanism.

Hand Feeding Your Dog and Another Dog

Do this with a dog that your dog knows. Feed the other dog and then your Ruff Love dog. Your dog will learn that by waiting his turn patiently, he will get rewards as well, possibly better treats than the other dog. You may want to start this with both dogs in a crate and then with the Ruff Love dog in a crate and the other dog loose. Next, try the Ruff Love dog loose and the other dog in a crate, and, finally, both dogs loose. The final step is to try this with a new dog. If at any time during this process your dog snaps at the other dog, take your treats away and go back to square one. Use praise only. Once you work up to both dogs being loose, be sure the dogs are further apart so that your puppy doesn't feel threatened by the presence of the other dog.

The in-depth study of aggression and how to deal with it is beyond the scope of this book. There are professionals to help you, and other books, such as *Dogs Are From Neptune* by Jean Donaldson, that are dedicated to the subject. It is in your dog's best interest to focus on overcoming his fears before you move forward with intense competitive sport training. In her book, *The Culture Clash,* Jean Donaldson states, "Social skills develop with repeated exposure but deteriorate with isolation." So, don't isolate your dog. Work through his fears and seek out professional help where your knowledge is limited.

Appendix Four
Ruff Love Quick Reference Charts

The charts on the following pages are a handy reference tool as they show you the complete progression of your Ruff Love program.

- The first chart is for the regular Ruff Love program.

- The second chart is for the modified Ruff Love for Puppies program.

Ruff Love Program Quick Reference Chart

Stage & Suggested Duration	The Crate	The Head Halter	Interaction with Other Dogs	Leashes & Long Lines	Off-Leash Free Time in Back Yard
Stage 1 7+ weeks	Dog in crate whenever unsupervised. Keep crate in the same room you're in if possible.	Wear for initial 3 days for 24 hours/day. After that, wear whenever out of crate.	On leash only, with one other household dog. Be sure to frequently call Ruff Love dog back to you for rewards.	Use whenever dog is out of crate.	Absolutely no off-lead free time outside.
Stage 2 3-5 weeks	Dog in crate at night or when left alone in house.	On when out of crate, but lead can be attached to regular collar except when near high distractions.	If he comes every time you call him, test him with a dog outside the household.	Use a light line inside. Use a long line outside. Fade if recall is good.	If he comes every time you call him, test him in new environments with light line on.
Stage 3 2-4 weeks	Dog sleeps in dog bed and is crated only when left alone in house.	On only when going to distracting area. Attach lead to regular collar.	Gradually allow interaction with all household dogs.	No line inside. Use light line outside only in new environments.	Dog is off leash but still only allowed outside when you are with him to supervise.
Stage 4 Lifetime of the dog	Crate is available if the dog chooses to use it.	Not necessary for the Ruff Love graduate.	Is left to interact with household dogs.	Use leash for security or reasons of good pet ownership.	As you choose. Most dogs will now choose to wait for you to join them for their fun.

Running with Other Dogs Outside	Toys Around the House	Availability of Chew Bones	Hand Feeding Meals	Relationship-Building Games	Individual Daily Training Schedule
No free running outside with other dogs.	Put the toy box away. No toys left out for unsupervised play.	Chew bones always available both in and out of crate.	The majority of meals are hand fed.	Work on hand targeting, Sit-Tug-Sit game, Gimme Dat Collar game, "side" and "close."	Many short sessions. Ideally, 3-8 sessions per day of 1-10 minutes duration.
If able to work on leash with other dogs running, test him on a light line outside with other dogs.	Work on tug-drop the toy test game to evaluate relationship.	Chew bones always available both in and out of crate.	Up to 75% of food ration for day can be fed in a bowl. Mix rest of food in with training treats or hand feed.	Continue games from Stage One. Add Tug-Drop the Toy, 1-2-3 game, and Hide & Seek game.	Continue with as many short sessions per day as possible. Ideally 3-5 per day.
Use this as a reward. Keep testing dog by calling him out of play.	Bring toy box back with one toy.	Chew bones always available both in and out of crate.	Mix kibble with training treats. Rest of meal fed in bowl.	Continue Tug-Drop the Toy and the 1-2-3 game. Expand Hide & Seek to large, unfamiliar areas.	One-on-one training not as critical. Always beneficial to work as many sessions as possible.
As you choose. Continue to occasionally call dog out of play.	Bring back the full toy box.	Chew bones always available both in and out of crate.	Only need to hand feed if your'e going to train that day.	Any that you can think of!	Your Ruff Love graduate may no longer require daily training unless he's a competition dog.

Ruff Love for Puppies Program Quick Reference Chart

Stage & Age of Puppy	The Crate	The Head Halter	Interaction with Other Puppies	Leashes & Long Lines	Off-Leash Free Time in Back Yard
Stage 1 7+ weeks	Puppy in crate whenever unsupervised. Keep crate in the same room you're in if possible.	First shape acceptance. At 10 weeks, wear for 3 days for 24 hours/day. After that, wear whenever out of crate.	Call the puppy back or use food lure on nose to draw puppy out of play frequently.	Use leash for training purposes. No need to use long line around the house for puppies.	Potty time on lead. Off leash with you to work recalls.
Stage 2 7+ months	Test freedom by leaving out of crate for 30 minutes without constant supervision. Crate him away from you.	On when out of crate, but lead can be attached to regular collar except when near high distractions.	If he comes every time you call him, he is allowed freedom with other puppies and dogs.	Lead or long line necessary only if puppy does not come the first time he is called.	Lead or long line necessary only if puppy does not come the first time he is called.
Stage 3 10+ months	Puppy sleeps in dog bed at night and is crated only when left alone in house.	On only when going to distracting area. Attach lead to regular collar.	Allowed to interaction with all household dogs.	Let the puppy's good behavior determine the amount of freedom he gets.	Puppy is off leash but still only allowed outside when you are with him to supervise.
Stage 4 14+ months	Crate is available if puppy chooses to use it.	May not be necessary for the Ruff Love graduate. Let your puppy's success dictate its use.	Is left to interact with household dogs.	Use leash for security or reasons of good pet ownership.	As you choose.

Running with Other Dogs Outside	Toys Around the House	Availability of Chew Bones	Hand Feeding Meals	Relationship-Building Games	Individual Daily Training Schedule
No free running outside with other dogs (for safety & training reasons). May work recall with other dogs around.	No toys left out for unsupervised play.	Chew bones always available both in and out of crate.	Work on puppy eating meals from his bowl as well as from your hand.	Work on hand targeting, Sit-Tug-Sit game, Gimme Dat Collar game, "side" and "close."	Many short sessions. Ideally, 3-8 sessions per day of 1-10 minutes duration. Start shaping behaviors and games.
If able to work on leash with other dogs running, progress to a light line when working with other dogs around.	Work on tug-drop the toy test game to evaluate relationship.	Chew bones always available both in and out of crate.	Use up to 75% of food portion for day as training rewards.	Continue games from Stage One. Add Tug-Drop the toy, 1-2-3 game, and Hide & Seek game.	Continue with as many short sessions per day as possible. Ideally 3-5 per day.
Use this as a reward. Keep testing puppy by calling him away from the other dogs to you while he is playing.	Bring out one toy.	Chew bones always available both in and out of crate.	As you choose.	Continue Tug-Drop the Toy and the 1-2-3 game. Expand Hide & Seek to large, unfamiliar areas.	Continue with as many short sessions per day as possible.
As you choose.	Bring out the full toy box.	Chew bones always available both in and out of crate.	As you choose.	Any that you can think of!	Your Ruff Love puppy graduate requires formal daily training only if you want to try performance dog sports.

For articles by Susan Garrett as well as information on Say Yes Dog Training Camps... There are several articles you will find useful in your Ruff Love training on the Say Yes website at www.clickerdogs.com. You will also find information there on our training camps. Alternatively, for information on camps, write to Say Yes Dog Training, 2780 Dunmark Rd., Alberton, Ontario, L0R 1A0, Canada.

For additional copies of this book or "Ruff Love" training supplies such as clickers, treats, tug toys, motivational toys, Gentle Leaders, and long lines... Visit www.cleanrun.com, call (800) 311-6503 within the U.S., call (413) 532-1389 outside the U.S., or write to Clean Run Productions, 17 Industrial Drive, South Hadley, MA 01075, USA. Clean Run also publishes a monthly magazine for dog agility enthusiasts, if you are interested in learning more about that sport.